God The Supreme Thought

Nkosinathi Ncala Jehovah Flow

Published by Nkosinathi Ncala Jehovah Flow, 2024.

GOD THE SUPREME THOUGHT

First edition. June 11, 2024.

ISBN: 979-8227691736

Written by Nkosinathi Ncala Jehovah Flow.

The Forsaken Truth – The Forbidden Lie.

What does it mean to be born?

What does it mean to live?

What does it mean to die?

What exists beyond these 3 realms?

How did we get to acquire knowledge on these 3 realms? Where does this wisdom come from? How do we attain this discernment?

Least who is the author of creation?

Existence is the continents' of life.

The pulse of creation is breath.

The images we perceive with the mind.

The thoughts we conceal in the heart.

The light we birth with the aid sight ignites the spheres of the imagination.

What separates ones thought from the next? Content.

The thoughts you allow into your mind willingly or unwillingly form part of your habit ultimately your belief system before you know it they inscribed into the very ideology aligned with your existence.

The Mind The Organism The Spirit

The Mind is the constitute and syntax of the gathering and organisation of words.

Sentences are structured language communication academia and industries advanced.

The organism the physical body the organs the blood that flows through the veins. This allows there to be mass and weight the human being is warm blooded has a heart and has a pulse and cast a living shadow.

The living shadow

Is that of a species that has life.

Life is breathe perhaps a dirty that has pours and oxygen and hydrogen flow through the nervous system.

The science of breath is life.

How many images can you capture in a minute? How many thoughts do you impart with during a single day?

When all is said and done what is the function of thought?

Did you live a life worth remembering?

Did you find eternal happiness in the things that bring you joy while you lived?

What matters the most to you in this lifetime? Is your life of any significance to it? What is the meaning of life to you really?

Where Can I Find The Truth?

Well that is subject to narration.

The location of the truth is remote.

You can not locate the truth on google maps you can use navigation software to pin point the bear truth.

The essence of life is narrated through interaction between man his natural environment and the interface bye of the intellectual realm.

When Can I Find The Truth?

Firstly let us ascertain what is it that you seek? What bought you to point where you leave your comfort zone an seek this reality?

When you find this state of existence what is it that you will deliberate?

When you find truth what is that you impart? Do you find peace?

The Truth You Seek.

The Concept of Peace?

Humanity has searched for peace since the befalling of intelligence and wisdom upon the dome.

How would you define peace?

As a utopia.

Space.

Defined boundaries where your time and inhabitants are at ease and comfort.

Perhaps The Truth You Seek Will Shatter Your Concept of Peace:

Perhaps you find out your life is still faithful you been married for 5 years you have 2 children she is hard working resourceful she is faithful yet she has fallen out love with you. You married too young.

You searched for peace you found it.

In contrast it was not joy it triggered your depression.

Where Can I Find The Truth?

Isolate subdue restrain constrain what ever situation you are facing. Come with open mind leave your fears behind. Truth is you can not forget your anxieties. Doubt is buried is the seat of the subconscious it is the very pyramid which consciousness was founded.

Take ownership of your life.

Where possible correct your mistakes.

Remember actions have eternal consequences. You live with today tomorrow. Can anyone forget yesterday?

Go ahead have a drink and another one and another one.

They say the truth will set you free?

What is the price you would pay to know the truth? Where do you buy the truth?

What is the price of the truth?.

Unfortunately the truth is not for sale.

Does anybody know where I can find the truth? I have searched in my heart it is deeper then the ocean fortunately I can not swim.

My mind is cluttered with over a trillion thoughts on a dull day.

Look no more trust child one day it will all make sense.

The Bible, Amen

The Content of a Image

Forms Consciousness:

What is that you see?

Did you hear that?

Can you smell that?

What did you say?

Father do you feel ME?

Man is alive.

Man is born.

Man lives.

Man dies.

Man is buried in a 6 foot grave, why I don't, know ask the undertaker.

While Man is alive.

Man shall thirst.

Man shall hunger.

Man shall reproduce.

Man is born in a hospital.

Man lives in the community.

Man attains a skills and spends the rest of his life shaping society for the future generations to come.

What consumes mankind while he is alive?

Survival.

Get a job.

Pay the bills.

Take care of the children's needs and their school fees.

Pay the rent.

Put cloths on your back.

Put food in the fridge.

Get a mode of transport.

Buy a home.

The Complex Nature of Relationships.

What came first love or hate?

Love and hate are primarily products of the primary instinct of survival within mankind fear.

Depending on the thoughts you keep.

Depending on the nature of your heart fear will manifest as love. Fear will manifest as hate.

The fruits of Love.

Faithfulness.

Patience.

Determination.

Dedication

Persistence.

Perseverance.

Fruits of Hate:

Jealousy.

Envy.

Greed.

Hatred.

Envy.

Thus mankind is divided.

Mankind has many tribes.

Is it necessary for the mind to have over 100 000 a day. We are not aware of the images that are entering our mind in a hourly basis. That is dangerous.

How is mankind to take stock of the true religion of man?

Will man kind ever unite in a lifetime?

We have over 200 countries.

At least over 2000 nations that speak in native tongues. We all for diversity.

Yet mankind growing further apart and we are going in an coarse that will split consciousness from serving the true God Jesus Christ for as long as we live.

Mild Hypnosis - The Keys To The Mind.

This Place Has No Name.

Pull yourself towards yourself and centre yourself. Close your eyes. Open your heart. Look inside your mind what do you see?

Keep the answer to yourself.

Do you like what you see?

If not what are you going to do about it?

What about the traits you can not change about yourself the fruits of the spirit.

You can advance your physical features should you have the finances. If you a bitter, jealousy, a liar, a cheat it will take some time to turn the other side of the soul, leaf or coin.

Now we will reverse psychology in play.

Now open your eyes.

Welcome back to reality.

Do you like what you see?

Again.

Never mind do not answer that.

Close your eyes.

Open your mind

Look inside your heart what is that you see? Then you see the light you are enlightened? When you saw the darkness did you not go blind?

Either way the power of your life force is in your hands. Never under estimate the drive attraction or repellent of will.

Now that you are in the presence of your inner being the core of your existence has been awakened. Regardless of he stance that your eyes are open are closed.

Your consciousness is now projecting from the seat of the imagination itself.

Creativity has been sparked. Where ever you command your mind it will heed.

There is no task too difficult to comprehend.

It took you 35 years to get to this place.

This place has no name. It is tranquil. Nor is it peace. Yet you have a total understanding of your existence and creator is that not what we are primaily born for?

You knocked.

You kicked down doors management would not let you in. Now you own a resort with all the resources in your world.

You have the keys to your mind.

They can not be lost.

They can not be misplaced.

They can not be cut.

They can not be copied.

Nor can they be cloned.

Yet the casualty of life is a constinent that governs all spheres of life.

There are only 2 physical attributes which can be taken away in reality by any circumstance. That would be birth and death. Life is a vessel of life and death.

As we exit this state of mild hypnosis.

Close your eyes.

You are surrounded by a sea of consciousness. You are some where in the middle of existence. Remember do no panic you are not alone. This place may not have a name.

Remember you are not alone.

Open your eyes welcome to reality.

What you have seen inside your heart and outside your mind if applied tactfully will help you navigate through the daily challenges and obstacles in life.

Mil Hypnosis - The Keys To The Mind.

This Place Has No Name.

A Poem By

Nkosinathi 2Pistolz Ncala

The Crucifixion of Negativity

The Rise of Faith.

Dedicated To The Cetyiwe Clan

Hymn Ocean Hill Song

Can you imagine a mind never touched by doubt. No hesitation. Your stance on survival is upright.Your intellectual capacity is majestic.

Your problem solving skills are elastic.

Your fabric is vintage you a classic you not plastic you can not be recycled you can not be replaced you go up in value even as you accumulate mileage.

27th March - Infinity.

This is the ideal space in the mind.

Within the circumference of consciousness. Exsistance is defined by the spirit the flesh the metaphysical and intellectual which branches of into AI.

What is fear?

Doubt, envy to seek what you do not possess materially and spiritually jealousy to be envious and greed is greedy by nature never happy or contempt with what you have.

Fear is an asylum.

Fear is a prison.

Fear is a fire run for your life.

Fear is being caught in the eye of a category 8 hail category storm with no refuge in sight. Fear is being trapped in the cycle of survival.

You spend your entire life chasing a dream. You working your entire life to retire at age 65. Who put that dream inside your mind.

Why can't you retire age 35?

With a basic salary of 25K and

4 additional incomes from your passions and dreams surpassing 100k for the for next 50 years of your life.

This is possible if so why not?

The pressure to provide is biblical and in these modern times highly stranious on the physical, mental health and spiritual health.

Fear helds the concept of freedom at random. Fear kept liberty in captivity with no trail. Fear tricked the mind into believing there is no hope faith has not been slay by your circumstances, rise.

Fear, slaughtered the consciousness with all its positive nature inserted negative thoughts. Resurrecting negativity.

Peace was crucified alive.

The spirit set on fire.

The soul is desolate troubled with no place to call home while it lives in the physical realm earth.

What will become of eternity.

If humanity stops believing in the concept of heaven, can you imagine the anarchy?

The chains would be set loose from Baal and the Clan of Lot Ammon an Moab.

Adultry and illicit sex is one sin that drives mankind away God from being in the mists of mankind physically and God surely will leave man's heart an presence eternally, please do not imagine.

A Poem By
Nkosinathi 2Pistolz Ncala

The Crucifixion of Fear - The Rise of Faith & Hope.

Fear - The Living Death.

Starve faith of hope and faith will die prematurely.

Fear is an insurgent.

A terrorist.

An agent of darkness.

The purpose of fear is to accelerate the process of anxiety. When thought is anxious it can not think clearly. Judgement is clouded. The mind the man are defeated and the battle is yet to begin.

Fear has influence on your next move.

Fear rattles thought.

Fear is venom to confidence.

Fear breeds being scared.

Fear will scar the perception you have of yourself, life and God.

Fear feeds the image and concept of your inferiority complex.

Fear is illusive you won't catch it an athlete. Fear is a scholar of your strengths and studies them and while you sleep your weaknesses besiege a coup ladies and gentlemen we have a new government in power we have taken over your mind. The only casualty is the ego.

You soul eternally belongs to the God that you serve. Yet as long as you live you a slave to survival.

We can not stop you from worshipping.

Praying.

Falling in love.

Getting married.

Having children.

What pains us your spirit and soul are still free even though they are trapped in the body and a slave to the concept of time and thought.

Your dreams are independent of time space and distance. You can be anything you want to be. Yes you can even align your divinity while you live with being an angel when your body nolonger casts a shadow.

Fear creates an illusion that today is hopeless. You alive today. Yet you concerned with ith tomorrow a concept which is an ancestor. Surely tomorrow will be awakened get the constinents of tomorrow's events remain a mystery.

Deal with today is it more critical then forever

Where guilt rise from?

Love would set you free?

Hate condemns you?

You alive yet your thoughts are occupied with death, that is not suicide, that is not depression that sick. Look in reality no matter how sad it may seem you have the gift of life you alive.

Does life out weigh death.

No one know what happens when you die, not for sure as far as I know.

So picture this.

You want to escape this life.

Your debt is too much.

You falling out of love with your wife.

You want to leave your job.

Today is murky you not an optimist your sceptical about tomorrow being sunny and rosey let alone a walk in the park.

You not sure where the spirit is located within the body. Yet you convinced the spirit is the breath of the soul. So you have made up your mind you leaving this earth by way of revolver on the left dome and a magnum force on the right dome.

You pull the trigger.

You left a broken heart.

Now your shadow will haunt you as long as you live in reality.

You are born you live you die.

Once you have been born.

Once you have lived.

Let us not get into the concept of death.

Once you have a birth certificate you will not escape the law of the land and commandments of the God.

Is It Possible To Kill The Spirit?

The basic answer is no you can't kill the spirit? Let us be controversial can you kill God? no. Energy in its purest form is omnipotent.

But then again why would you want to kill the spirit? Should is the state of consciousness plotting to assonate the spirit? Do you have death on your mind? Do you have blood on your hands?

Have you transgressed God?

Have you committed a sin?

Have committed a crime?

The crime is in the hands of the jury.

Should you have committed a sin you accountable to God, remorse comes with forgiveness.

Yet the spirit is not of the flesh.

It ascends and dwells in your body while you live and it exists after your last breath the spirit is eternal.

The spirit is not a parasite or bacteria.

It does not use the host for its food blood and nutrients it guides you and leads you to get closer to God.

Is there a difference between the spirit and the soul? No body knows for sure.

Could the spirit be your breath. The soul could be the very air that you breath?

Where is the spirit located?

What is the image of the soul?

Is the spirit born physically?

Can the soul die conceptually?

Are the spirit and soul exempt of death?

What exists above thought?

May I ask you a silly question how do you know that you are alive?

Well.

You are you breathing.

You projecting consciousness.

You have dreams.

And you living within reality.

Extracts of survival.

Stress induced by the pressures of survival. The rent is due. Bill's must be payed. The debt takes a toll on our credit score happiness and ultimately wholes tic well being.

When you are alive. Yet the reason you were born. Perhaps it's taking you too long to find the purpose of your existence.

Technically you can not kill the soul.

Yet you can frustrate the soul by making the host of the soul the human being dependent on a guardian lover or parent beyond adolescent.

Manipulation and control can never be a good thing even in moderation. You can not kill the soul. Yet you can make life so unbearable that the quality of life is inhuman.

You alive yet you a living dead dream.

Is it possible to kill the soul, No.

Yet you can depresses it state of mind clinically in this lifetime.

Is It Possible To Kill The Spirit, NO.

Nkosinathi 2Pistolz Ncala

How Did The First Thought Manifest In The Human Mind?

Divine intervention?

Is thought man made?

Is thought a process of animals and species evolving?

What is the destiny of thought?

Is the fate of thought independent from the fate of man?

Creatures of creation give birth.

They nurture the young till they can fend for themselves. Yet humanity has evolved beyond the circumference of our natural habitat. Humanity has industrialised the concept of nature.

Currency has corrupted the nature of goodness. In 2024 the heart is ruled by greed, envy and jealousy the fall of virtue.

We need money to survive. In the modern society. The fact remains. After you have fought the battle called life when all is said and done money is not a natural resource.

So the establishment of the faculty of currency who is really benefiting? The expropriation of the natural resources of mother earth while the people of the land remain impoverished.

How long can the famine of poverty and suffering be allowed to stunt?

Why does life come to an end?

We are born to live out our dreams into reality. Why do we have to die. The flesh grows old and meets its demise.

Flesh of my flesh. Ashes to ashes and dust to dust. Bones will be consumed by maggots.

Mankind wants to live forever.

Mankind attained understanding..

Mankind's discernmenti transcended the boarders of the physical realm.

Mankind is an explorer.

Mankind transcends times zones.

Mankind builds space ships and transcends out of space.

Yet the some animal species which existed before mankind's rise are extinct if not on the endangered list. Our forests are being cut alarming rates so we can print more money so we can buy more furniture for homes and wood grain for our exotic cars.

The state of the ozone layer is a floor in our understanding of the importance of the balance of natural forces of nature. As well a bee is no less important then an ant.

Is man made purely of flesh.

Earth existence when the spirit can nolonger carry the flesh.

Where does knowledge ascend from?

Yes wisdom is experience examination repetition and improving existing processes and systems.

So there is nothing beyond existence.

Reality is the pinnacle of existence.

Survival which is man made the 9 - 5

Is purely there to pay your bills. Comfort is a luxury are for the nobles. Poverty is a reality for the masses of the population.

Look around you nature was created by the force of existence the universe.

Without mankind the universe existence evolves and thrives without twitching or losing a limb.

Without the universe mankind would not even be a memory. Mankind would have have been given the opportunity to be adorned with a name and inherit a surname. Without nature mankind wouldn't be able to breath let alone to be born into the physical realm.

Mankind can not evolve without the universe. Mankind is conceived into nature. Thought manifests into the world of the natural elements wood, fire, water, air, gold, platinum, silver and gold.

A Poem By:

Nkosinathi 2Pistolz Ncala

The Nature of God:
As Benedict Bach Spinza said
God Is Nature.
Dutch Philosopher 16th century.
True.
Man can not live off the bread alone.
Verily man must abide by the word.
The creator of the universe and life.
God Lord Jesus Christ.
The flesh shall perish.
Sure there is insurance.
Yes there is life cover.
Yet when you a diagnosed with a chronic illness and your medical aid has been exhausted. When your taxes now outweigh your income due to none compliance.
When you lose your job.
You wife takes her due half.
You had no children that is what strained the relationship. You you remarried. She also left you. You had commitment issues she also took the other half.
Now you clinically depressed.
Whats left?
Love is its a feeling.
Primarily live is between parent and child.
The love between man and woman often falls to desire and nature of temptation.
Love is brittle, yet love is the symbol of unity and is beautiful.
The body ages and gets weak.
Money comes and go..
When your back is against the wall what keeps you alive?

When dark clouds rise and you can not see the sunshine and it's been raining so long you wish it would stop. Only to find out a drought is coming for the next year.

When your enemy rises up against you.

And you are weaker then them.

Do you lean on your own understanding?

Do you turn to God Jesus Christ.

Do you turn to the universe which is a reflection of the glory and creation of God? Do you turn to science?

Do you turn to yourself?

So what is the spirit?

The nature of your God.

What is the soul?

Your shadow in the spiritual world.

Your ego is the seat of your consciousness.

Your imagination is the crown of your existence creativity is of the essence.

What is the flesh?

A reflection of the glory of your creation.

Take care of your temple you are a reflection of God. Please do not let that image overwhelm you. We were created in the image of the Gods.

Nkosinathi 2Pistolz Ncala

Salvation:

What is salvation?

What is the meaning of Salvation

Romans 10 verse 8 - 11.

But what saith it? The word is nigh thee, even in thy mouth, and in thy heart: that is, the word of faith, which we preach;

That if thou shalt confess with thy mouth the Lord Jesus, and shalt believe in thine heart that God hath raised him from the dead, thou shalt be saved.

For with the heart man believeth unto righteousness; and with the mouth confession is made unto salvation.

For the scripture saith, Whosoever believeth on him shall not be ashamed.

—Romans 10:8-11

KJV Holy Bible https://bibliacomigo.page.link/DtUc

Nobody knows when it's their time to go.

When it is your time to go to eternity.

Who will fetch your soul?

Do you believe in judgement day?

Do you believe in the fate of the righteous? Who judges the heathens?

The tricky mathematical equation about the moment of death.

What matter most?

Your current state of affairs.

Your net worth is essential to your estate.

Your debtors will take what is due to them.

Life goes on after your death.

The manner in which your family lived while your alive. Did you give your children the skills to fend for themselves? Did you leave them a substantial inheritance even that can be depleted in a matter on months or years it's a matter of when how and time.

Upon death.

Does God call your soul at the moment your heart stops beating.

Could it be true that by that very moment of deliberation when God summons your spirit back to its creator your fate has been decided.

Why would God call your soul back to heaven and leave the body to die a natural death on earth and the spirit just like your shadow live on forever.

The lessons on earth can not be taken for granted. Learn your lessons master your plan. Do not be easily distracted. Find something worth living for and pursue it till it becomes a living dream.

Lord.

Oh Lord God Jesus Christ.

Keep my salvation till it's time to go Heaven

Thought Projecting Consciousness Into Reality:

Can you tell the difference between reality and survival? Can you can the difference between a truth and a lie?

What draws mankind towards a nature of goodness? What draws mankind towards darkness? The thoughts we keep.

What is the content of thought?

Memories.

Experience.

Data information reflecting on past analysing our mistakes and making us better human beings. An unexamined life is a life not worth living.

How does consciousness perceive reality. How does reality perceive a dream? Fundamentally speaking is there a difference between a dream and reality?

The world of reality and the realm of dreams essentially could be a continuation of the other.

How does the mind project consciousness into existence?

Idealistically the content of consciousness is thought images and perception.

How long does it take an average human being to discover what is the meaning of life? Once you have made peace with adversity. Let us ascertain what are you going to do with your gift of life? How much time do you have on earth? No one knows for sure but God.

Can happiness be taken away from you?

Is joy not a permanent state of consciousness? Does laughter echo only in the moment. Birth is lived. Could death be a eternal heaven.

When you are faced with obstacles what do you do? What do you fear? And why?will you meet your demise with fear on your mind?

On that fateful day the angels call your name are you judged on your final thoughts? Are you judges on the transgressions of your entire life leading to your final thought

Can you differentiate between thought and consciousness? Thought is pure energy which is refined to form the conscious form the instrument of consciousness itself.

What is the distance between two thoughts? What is the weight of a single thought what is the mass of an motive?

What is the gravity of deception?

What happens to a dead thought?

What happens to a dying motive?

What is the fate of a lie being born?

What carnation does the truth have on life?

When does an ideology graduate from mind to reality? How long on average will that process take? Thought is groomed in the mind and expresses itself in reality.

Thought Projecting Consciousness Into Reality:

How Is Consciousness Perceived Through The Eye of The Mind?

So we has established the mind is alive.

The mind broadcasts thoughts through the nervous system causing consciousness to cast into projection life takes form of breath.

Fragments of perception form images.

Images are transcripts which conglomerate from the gathering of pictures coming alive through motion space distance and time.

Consciousness is subcategorised into forces of instinct, leisure and run from the pain. Thus man is conflicted terror rains on the street. The coffers of treasury are swindled on a scale of poaching yet the federals are accountable to nobody but themselves.

Mankind primary motive while we alive we seek desire and we run from pain.

Primary the mind is developing naturally without even being aware of it our intellectual DNA Genetics and fingerprints form before our first thought comes alive.

By the time we are given a name and surname your identy has been labelled.

What is the process of labelling? Why is association so important? Categorising.

Emotions: anger anxiety hate resentment aggression leading to violence penatimately.

Feelings:

Joy happiness jubilation love.

These are primarily instincts which have formed in the mind. Shaping thought. Ideologies form.

Intelligence is born.

Stupidity mutates into foolishness and arrogance the opposite of confidence.

Are you getting a clearer picture of the Psychology of Thought?

Now that the mind has an identity and thought is alive and well.

We get biblical.

Mankind is given free WILL.

What is wrong verses should I do what is right? Should I go left should I go right?

Should I stand still? You can take your thought anywhere in the world. You can picture a living dimension which is yet to form and bring it life.

Put pen and paper use your table and later design a app and bring your vision to life. The prospects of the mind are infinite.

Nkosinathi 2Pistolz Ncala

The Biology of Thought:

Thought is unipolar.

Motive is tripolar.

Consciousness is octave.

Sin will ultimately dig you an early grave.

Our actions are aligned with understanding.

Our deeds may be the rise of disobeying the commandments of God and the law.

Then comes the disciplines of reasoning.

Righteous.

Virtue.

Sin.

Judgement.

Reasoning.

Repentance.

Forgiveness

Remorse

Gratitude.

Grace follows you independent of your efforts.

By association we build memory.

To remember is a pyramid in how the mind builds recognition and growth the cognitive side of the brain. Never take for granted your ability to recall it is an essential pillar to awakening enlightenment.

Align today with the now.

Can you make peace with the past if yesterday is dead. Tomorrow is yet to take its first breath. Where can I find peace. The fallacy war is aggression and somewhere in the story line compassion met an unnatural demise.

Perhaps to doubt the existence of supreme consciousness is the fallacy to leer the existence of God. What is left of the higher self without the existence of a deity?

May we indulge what is the primary purpose of thought?

Reality is the natural environment which mankind procreates reproduces navigates feeds and cloths his young.

Survival is a sub category of existence which primary is a creation of mankind leaning on wisdom knowledge and his own understanding. The fruits of survival are industrialisation primarily. AI Artificial Intelligence is the cloning of thought digitally and figuratively speaking.

Money is the root of all suffering.

Laziness is a lack of drive and motivation perhaps even a stint of depression.

Saddens is a state of sulleness morose glitches of a broken heart.

The mind is the place where mankind advances his plans for humanity the earth an all that lies within the known universe.

One of these days when made it to heaven. Some wise brothers riding on a colt ass (biblically speaking curses) will try conqure the highest regime in the history of existence.

There is nothing new under the sun

Nkosinathi 2Pistolz Ncala

The Descendants of Time:

Birth.

Life &

Death.

In order to live to have been born.

In order to die you need to have lived.

Life the word was born in the mind and concealed in the heart. Knowledge wisdom discernment and understanding stung from the word.

Language yet why does mankind have so many tongues. Would it not have been simpler if mankind had one primary language as a matter of fact we would advance more rapidly as a species instead we bickering who is God's Chosen race.

There is one God.

We are his creation.

Yes there are many nations due exploring and settlers and so on and so on.

Yet humanity we are one race.

We are Gods people.

We are divided by geographical location.

Class.

Status.

The State of Mind Address:

What Is Your Perception of Reality?

I would say it depends on how you look at it. How do you see reality? Verses the was it actually.

Things aren't always what they seem.

Space, Time Distance & Gravity

These Elements Regulate The Human Mind.

Space is the distance between 2 places simultaneously measured primarily from point A to B. With space there is a geographical location a land mass variation calculated in kilometres measured in distance variables.

Kilograms is the density of mass is weighed by a scale. Anything that has mass casts a shadow the law of weight.

Time is the measurement of the planets as they orbit the earth. Watching as thoughts enter and leave to mind. Leaving a footprint of positive and negative thoughts.

Some thoughts are calculated organised.

Some thoughts are sporadic neither headed left neither headed right.

There is no instrument to measure their aptitude. Neither is their fate in Gods hands. Their destiny is in limbo unknown.

Man is accountable for what ever thoughts enter his mind. What are the channels thought enter the mind? Conversation dreams and nightmares. When the mind is in 5 states conscious unconscious subconscious aware and unaware.

Ultimatly you are defined by the thoughts you keep.

Man is the author of the thoughts in his mind. Mankind lives with the consequences of the thoughts that leave his mind shaping his immediate reality.

What is the texture of thought?

The fabric of thinking.

Clothing the mind.

The key to the mind is to displace fear.

The door to the heart is to confront motive and enlighten darkness.

The seat of the soul on earth is the spirit.

The enemy is the thoughts we keep.

Thoughts are neutral in the mind primarily. At what point in the lifespan of the thought does thought take the form of a negative thought or a positive thought?

The intentions and motives which surround thought shape and mould thought into the ideologies they manifest matter over mind.

Aggression is frustration. Unresolved grief. Low esteem doubt and limited understanding of one's self worth.

Anger rage and violence are the final acts of desperation when the centre which controls emotions and stimuli in the mind has collapsed.

Gravity is a neutral magnatic field neither negative nor positive.

Gravity is the centre of existence neutralizing negative and positive particles is mass and energy concurrently.

What Is Your Perception of Reality?

I would say it depends on how you look at it. How do you see reality? Verses the was it actually.

Things aren't always what they seem.

A Poem By

Nkosinathi 2Pistolz Ncala

How Energy Comes Alive:

Consciousness can not be born.

Consciousness can not die.

Then precisely how does consciousness come into existence?

Consciousness is converted into energy.

Does consciousness reproduce?

So primarily for consciousness to exist there are 2 strands a male strand and a female strand.

Gods Weapons of Mass Creation:

Consciousness.

Energy.

Gravity.

Velocity.

Mass.

Time was conceived and the mind was perceived.

The Reflection of Light Is Consciousness's in essence primarily.

Darkness Is The Force of Gravity:

Light has no mass it is transparent see through like the air.

When the light shines through the darkness the spectrum forms, colour is born. Through consciousness we perceive the world.

The source of light is the sun.

The image is the entity fixed object.

Where does the light originate?

Where does darkness come from?

How did it take for the sun to form?

Did the moon was moon and the exhaust before time?

We can expropriate darkness and light gave rise to time.

Time is consciousness.

Time is the eye of the universe.

Time is the heart of existence.

Time is the mind if thought.

Time is a mystery.

Time is alive.

Yet is has no physical perimeter.

The circumference time reaches can not be measured by any means reasonable.

Time is not confined by the law of gravity. Time has no weight yet it is a potentially destructive force.

Time has 2 spheres mechanical time and biological time. Yet primarily time is not Man made. Is time the only living entity that existence independent of Gods creation. Time alternatively could be God.

A Poem By
   Nkosinathi 2Pistolz Ncala

Spirit of A Living Cat

A cat has 9 lives.

Why would a cat have 9 lives?

The cat is very peculiar mysterious.

Eager to climb a tree walk on the highest branch fall 90 feet only to land on its feet.

3 days later gain the courage to climb the same tree walk on the thinnest branch and walk across the entire circumference of the tree like it did not mean anything at all the kitty did not even break a sweat.

The baby kitten is innocent and cute.

Yet the cat by nature has the human mind it is cunning and curious like the serpent and the human being.

In ancient Egypt cat Goddess Bassett as the primary symbol of fertility and other cats watching the tombs of the nobles and Pharaoh mummy's buried in the Egyptian pyramids keeping evil spirits away.

So the misconception amongst Africans that cats are evil is misconstrued. If cats in ancient days at the height of human understanding when God first appeared to man and let his commandments known humanity.

Cats were the interface between the spirit world and the world of the living.

Let us examine the nine lives of the cat:

1. The kitty is born.

2. The cat lives a mortal life.

3. The cat dies a natural death.

4. The cat is born as a dead spirit.

5. The cat becomes a dead spirit living amongst the living on earth.

6. The cat dies 1st spiritual death.

7. The cat is born again lives dies 2nd spiritual death.

8. The cat is born again dies 3rd spiritual death.

9. The cat dies its final death becomes a living spirit an angel from heaven ascended into earth or a dead spirit eternally living amongst the living.

This is the spiritual reason why they say a cat has 9 lives.

Beware be cognisant of superstitions.

Spread the gospel.

Worship the true God Jesus Christ.

Be weary of pyramid schemes.

Before you sell your soul remember Money won't but you a seat in Heaven.

Nkosinathi 2Pistolz

Then Spirit of The Dead Cat

These cats have competed the cycle of the 9 lives of a cat.

Let us examine the nine lives of the cat:

1. The kitty is born.

2. The cat lives a mortal life.

3. The cat dies a natural death.

4. The cat is born as a dead spirit.

5. The cat becomes a dead spirit living amongst the living on earth.

6. The cat dies 1st spiritual death.

7.The cat is born again lives dies 2nd spiritual death.

8. The cat is born again dies 3rd spiritual death.

9. The cat dies its final death becomes a living spirit an angel from heaven ascended into earth or a dead spirit eternally living amongst the living.

The dead cat is dangerous.

It can read thoughts.

Yes it can read human being thoughts.

The dead cat is primarily a reflection of the darkness. It can only merge and supplement with negative thoughts.

Thus when you are surrounded with cats that are restless as though they are suckling on milk although fully grown. Making suspicious witchery baby noises at awkward hours of the morning never during broad day light.

Know there is a spiritual battle manifesting. The cries of babies is actual children or spirits trapped in a abyss in the belly of a pregnant serpent crying to God for salvation.

Take heed of the lessons life has taught you. Be faithful in your heart keep your words alive. May the Bible be your reference point when you faced with an obstacle.

Mourn in good times you shall rejoice in times of strife and hardships.

A Poem By
Nkosinathi 2Pistolz Ncala

The Dying Serpent
Is the spirit of a living man.
The dying serpent has the mind of a wicked full grown man that once lived failed as a human being and wants to settle the score.
Can read minds.
Yet the dying serpent can not intercept positive thoughts.

Nkosinathi 2Pistolz Ncala

The Dead Serpent

Is a spirit yet to be born.

Motives yet to form.

A mind born with no form.

Not all serpents are evil.

Some are born devils.

Some will be angels.

What fascinates God with serpents?

Lucifer & his legions.

The fall of heaven.

The Garden of Eden.

Consciousness is independent of thought. You can not tame motive.

Thought incretion will not hypnotise a mind that is alert.

Anything cold blooded can not be trusted. Anything cold blooded can not naturally be domesticated the hour you turn your back on it your loved one will be devoured.

A cold blooded entity can not be trusted period. Reptilians are the bloodline of Luciferians the tribe of Baal.

Judgement of The Living Is In Procession

God Jesus Christ speaks in Parables.

A serpent is a fallen angel it has derestriction and preliminary judgement over the living on earth till it's time to go to heaven.

A animal that is eaten by a serpent.

Has manifested to the lowest level in the animal kingdom. The animal may be a rat, rabbit, fowl.

Can you see the danger of animals eating beef, lamb, goat. Yes these animals were unblemished and sacrifices in the old testament yet essentially they are living human souls.

The soul of that animal is a human beings soul and spirit.

A animal eaten by a male serpent shall be condemned to death according to their transgressions in their current lifetime.

A animal eaten by a pregnant female serpent. The spirit and soul of the human being shall be incarnate into her eggs which she birthed and she will watch over them till they are born.

Remember a serpent is born all knowing.

We have 12 arch angels roaming the earth at any given time.

144 000 legions are born everyday.

The battle for the soul has began.

A Poem By Nkosinathi 2Pistolz Ncala

Man Is Created In The Image of God

Speak.

A Dog is Created In The Image of Man

Bark

In the beginning was the word and the word was God.

Hoof

Man if God's best friend.

A Dog is a a Man's best friend.

A Cat is a dog's Best Friend.

Thought Sent A Tweet To God Rising Hell Amongst The Arch Angels:

(The Birth of The God Child).

At Birth a child named Thought.

The meaning of God's last born God Child, Thought.

The ability to picture imagine create and breathe life into life. A place uniting dreams minds & matter.

Curses are words mixed with piss swear words lies and profanity were uttered on earth. What transpires on earth reflects in the realm of Heaven.

The curse words they landed on the alter.

An unblemished bullock lay in a catatonic state.

The Gods waited 1 000 years for the birth and raising of this cuffing. The time is now 465 857 BC GC

Heaven's Layer

The outer core.

A view of universe the sun the moon the Stars galaxies the milky way and yes planet and hell.

The middle layer.

Security the pearly gates screening of souls who were human and are to be initiated as angels.

The inner core.

Where Angels and worshiping takes place.

The nucleus where the Gods reside.

The unknown realm.

Where Gods reproduce.

Behold Son of Man a God is Born.

One day you will be human only for a little while. A God is born with understanding the moment umbilical cord is separated from the placenta.

For security reasons a Godchild is born not knowing their mother. The tail of sin has a head called a snake. It is written crush the head of a serpent mankind heel has already been bruised.

Now back to the delimit the ultimate comfort transgression and peace offering for the young God has been blemished

Angels and Arch angel may mediate look him in the eyes through telekinesis telepathy thought projection they travel to eternity while in Heaven and secure the destiny of the God Child it is on earth.

Angels gather wings trumpets harps colt asses stallions medallions Chaldeans.

Heaven is wagering a war against Satan not a single weapon in sight.

144 000 angels.

8 billion legions a army of swine's.

Enough arsnary to blow up the earth in 2 days.

God is no where in sight.

Lucifer is in gauging in illicit sex illicit narcotics with earthly Goddess. This enrages God infuriating the elders.

Using insight God comes down realising Lucifer plays dirty. This is not a war to be fort. This is not a war to be lost. This is a war to be won. A stalemate would give too much ground and power to the legion swine's.

Lucifer's son is born in secret.

The more filth the stronger Lucifer get.

The Holy and spiritual the people and honesty in prayer and worship gives God Hosanna supreme peace.

The essence of creation is humanity. Humanity is essentially God's heart.

The Supreme Thought God.

What is God's chalice?

How does God prepare for warfare?

Is God a might warrior?

Has God ever been defeated in war?

Gods first defeat:

The fall of the first angel in Heaven lucifer he left with too much information on the kingdom, perhaps in blind sight hindsight God never saw this betrayal coming.

What is Gods arsnary?

As far as history tells as the source of Heavens head aches is one.

Code name Blasphemy and a swine and legions.

Yet on the kingdom of earth.

Behold there cometh the son of man.

Son of God Jesus Christ.

The Jesus - Judas effect.

It was written the betrayal and prophesied. God the kingdom and the angels were eternally prepared after the God - Debarcle.

A Poem By

Nkosinathi 2Pistolz Ncala

Man Is Created In The Image of God

The birth of the Luciferian Child named

Idol.

We won't indulge into the oaths.

Human sacrifices. Blood tithes. Not to undermine the Luciferians they really not that smart.

They flip everything upside down.

Turn a circle around it is still a circle.

Turn a triangle upside down it is still a triangle.

The key is to know your bible.

Beware of what dwells in your heart.

Have utter control of what enters your mind. Regulate thought. Let nothing out that will tarnish your reputation.

Judgement Day:

Is the day the spirit lives eternally in Heaven. God forbid the spirit dies and burns in Hell for eternity.

For the sake of creation God and Lucifer not face come face to face at least in the interim.

500 000 BC GC

Idol and Thought

Luciferian and God Child come face to face.

Till then Brethren keep the faith.

Lucifer cometh like a thief in the night.

Not to steal but to kill and destroy.

Invest not in God which rusts and is eaten by moth. Keep your salvation safe with God our Lord Jesus Christ.

Ok the year 500 000 BC GC

3 days before the 17th of August.

Thought had a dream. In his eyes he was being visited by an alien.

Thought was near a river it was flowing and calm. The strange creature human features yet rather lean and average height.

He called him by his name in the dream.

The God Child did not reply.

He called him the second time.

He responded how do you know my name. He could not utter a word he could not lie.

The 3rd time he called his same he was drawn to him like a magnet.

He used his magnetic field to naturally repel.

God sensed the God Child was in troubled. Asked the Guardians at the Palace in Houghton South Africa where the was. He is fast asleep dreaming father. He was now the age 33 you can imagine why God was anxious.

The alien seemed weak.

Yet when the enemy seems well he is strong. When is he perceived as far he is close. The Art of War.

When Thought was close enough to touch at arms length idol the Luciferian took 3 deep breaths they smelt like death

The forth breath swallowed a part of me they he crackled hackled laughed and vanished its as though he took my soul.

Come down thought Lucifer has no children the only person that could do that is Lucifer's Son.

I try reach heaven's land line telepathically, I dial the pager line, I make contact with Dad's cellular no network WTF that's an alarm God hears Thought God Childs distress and sends guardians to aid my distress.

A journey that would have taken 3 hours.

took 18 hours.

Tonight God is on earth Houghton Estate.

Security is so tight it's underground.

There is not a fly on the wall.

The dogs are not allowed to bark.

After examining the event.

The elders deliberate.

Thought the God Childs soul, spirit and conscious has been snatched by an unknown entity highly unlikely.

When God head was born he had no Luciferian Child. That was the last time he was allowed on earth in ound unchained from 1000 mile bottomless and void pit to cause havoc and mislead the weak in faith only for a little while because only him and God know the day of judgement.

The elder on of elder screams

Oh My God.

God replies as in the EMOJI OMG

No Father.

Remember the night Thought the God Child it as born and we came to earth.

Lucifer was having a party. Yes sex drugs alcohol nothing there.

This party took place in Ethiopia

there were princess and goddess Caucasian and African.

God who you think one of the Goddess was Sheba

Queen Sheba

God replies to the Elders

OMG

The elders respond

As in Oh My God

God says no the EMOJI

OMG

They chuckle.

A Poem By

Nkosinathi 2Pistolz Ncala

What Is The Highest Level of Consciousness Thought Can Reach?

Well let us have a look at the spectrum of thought. The highest thought is being closeness (oneness) with God.

Closeness (oneness) with God what does that really mean? The death of the ego. To let go of the self. A daily renewal through prayer mediation reading the Bible repenting and not sinning again as far as possible.

Most importantly keeping an eye on your salvation.

States of consciousness:

Innovative and creating something from nothing, alchemy. Building sectors of academia engineering building roads and bridges. Science and technology Artificial Intelligence advances in medicine health care and education.

Imagination manifesting from mind to matter, reality. Creativity the arts drama sports movies documentaries acting.

Creatives.

Pressures of survival:

Depression clinical sadness can lead to suicide.

The Prism of Consciousness.

The 2 magnetic fields which breathe energy to life exhaling consciousness.

Primarily darkness and light

are the 2 magnetic forces in nature

which creation abides from.

Light and darkness are in equilibrium.

There was neither day or night in the beginning. Existence was void.

Time was yet to tick.

Time and life were yet to cross paths.

The sun light existed before the first moon rose. The light blinds the darkness.

Consciousness awareness awakens from this state. Day and night were born.

Till this day more then 3 billion years since day and night danced at dawn.

The moment.

The present.

The now is all we really have.

Tomorrow is a concept of worry.

Tomorrow is an ideology of anxiety.

If we pay due diligence to the present.

There is no need to be anxious about the future. Tomorrow consumed todays energy. Be present today.

If you focus on too much tomorrow fear creeps in you next few moves may be sloppy now tomorrow is suspect.

Just as the mind exists independent of consciousness. The earth and water are the primarily the darkness and light of planet earth.

We have established in order for the process of reproduction process to take place. For procreation, intimacy for a child to be born

for the spirit to be conceived there has to be a same species a male force and a female force.

Mating consensually.

Thus the sperm can germinate with the ovary and the process of procreation manifests.

The moment of climax between man and woman is probably the most out of world experience and sensation to the release of endorphins adrenaline and other hormones.

Yet sex naturally without stimulants after the age of 40 1 to 3 encounter per encounter depending on your libido should be sufficent.Yet this is not cast in stone this vary from individual to individual.

Climatology what is the sensation when the weather is hot when the weather is hot what sensation you get?

Some people are depressed when the weather is hot .

Some people are happy when the weather is cold.

What you see as pretty may be unattractive to me.

What you fear may be my fetish.

In retrospect life is relative yet resolute and constant, change is a variable that is in equilibrium.

Human behaviour modification.

Variables human beings are born with a soul which harbours the spirit and your host is the human body.

You are given an identity at birth.

You are classified a boy or girl.

You are either male or female.

The male will fend for the family.

The female is fertile and will give birth to the children.

Humanity has followed this prototype for at least the past 6 000 years.

There have been religious wars.

There have been masses of mass distraction. Migrants, Xenophobia, Tsunamis, Forest fires, Ozone Layer Breaches, Cultural Supremacy.

Now the human mind is perverted the is human trafficking we are on the brinks of moral extinction Sodom and Gomorrah all over again. Mankind with all this intelligence when will we ever learn.

What are your top 5 inventions that propelled humanity to the next dimension since the beginning of time.

1. The wheel.

2. The clock.

3. Pen and paper.

4. The internet GPS.

5. The motor car transport.

What are top 5 ingredients to mankind's downfall:

1. Racism.

2. Sin.

3.Lack of Remorse.

4. Repentance and Forgiveness is exhaled.

5. Man does not believe in himself how can he believe in God?

A Poem By

Nkosinathi 2Pistolz Ncala

To Higher Levels of Consciousness Analysis And Observation of One's Behaviours.

Are you aware of the thoughts you keep?

What is the nature of your thought?

Do you believe in virtue?

Are you living for the day?

Facing the unpleasant inevitables.

What matters the most to you?

Inevitably adversity will snatch the grasp of your palm from it how does that reality make you feel?

Can thought reason beyond the confines of consciousness?

What is consciousness?

Energy confined within a space a prism called the mind. Within the mind lies segments of fields of energy divided into memories which consciousness will be streamlined and magnify into sectors of thoughts instincts and desires.

From consciousness we have dreams polar effect nightmares. Delicts of thought Alzheimer's and issues and the stigma of mental health.

So we have established consciousness is independent of the mind. Yet they co exist for the organism to function and survive in reality.

Consciousness is biological..

Stress is mechanical a product of survival habitually there is famine in the land and animal or mankind can not pay the bond he just lost his job.

Stress is natural.

Stress is a force of nature.

Stress is neural primary at a glance neither positive or negative.

Yet stress unexamined can collapse the entire nervous system without an army and a coup. Stress is the dangerous by any imaginable extreme.

Pay close attention to the events in your life that may stress you. Study your mistakes that is the indigenous way to grow and turn tragedy into lessons, that is of the essence primitive importance.

Pressure is a force exerted internally.

Pressure is a force exerted externally.

Pressure is a force at the core of the organism biologically and intellectually.

Your inability to cope with pressure.

Your coping skills of pressure determine weather you will survive.

The underline the truth if the matter weather you will surpass the maindaine and great like those that came before you your ancestors.

What are the barriers to the development of thought? What enhances the advances of the ideology of thought propergating intellectual stimuli.

Primary 9 Fields of thought:

Academia.

Sports.

Politics.

Religion.

Criminology

The Judetary.

The Prison System and

Health care system.

The education system.

Analytical Intelligence

A Poem By

Nkosinathi 2Pistolz Ncala

Thought Sent A Tweet To God Raising Hell Amongst The Arch Angels:

(The Birth of The God Child).

At Birth a child named Thought.

The meaning of God's last born God Child, Thought.

The ability to picture imagine create and breathe into life. A place uniting dreams minds & matter.

Curses are words mixed with piss sear words lies and profanity were uttered on earth. What transpires on earth reflects in the realm of Heaven.

The curse words they landed on the alter.

An unblemished bullock lay in a catatonic state.

The Gods waited 1 000 years for the birth and raising of this cuffling. The time is now 465 857 BC GC

Heaven's Layer

The outer core.

A view of universe the sun the moon the Stars galaxies the milky way and yes planet and hell.

The middle layer.

Security the pearly gates screening of souls who were human and are to be initiated as angels.

The inner core.

Where Angels and worshiping takes place.

The nucleus where the Gods reside.

The unknown realm.

Where Gods reproduce.

Behold Son of Man a God is Born.

One day you will be human only for a little while. A God is born with understanding the moment umbilical cord is separated from the placenta.

For security reasons a Godchild is born not knowing their mother. The tail of sin has a head called a snake. It is written crush the head of a serpent mankind heel has already been bruised.

Now back to the dilemma the ultimate comfort transgression and peace offering for the young God has been blemished

Look him in the eyes through telekinesis telepathy thought projection they travel to eternity while in Heaven and secure the destiny of the God Child it is on earth.

Angels gather wings trumpets harps colt asses stallions medallions Chaldeans.

Heaven is waging a ear against Satan not a single weapon in sight.

144 000 angels 8 billion legions.

An army of swine's.

Enough arsnary to blow up the earth in 2 days.

God is no where in sight.

Lucifer is in gauging in illicit sex illicit narcotics with earthly Goddess. This enrages God infuriating the elders.

Using insight God comes down realising Lucifer plays dirty. This is not a ear to be fort. This is not a war to be lost. This is a war to be won. A stalemate would give too much ground and power to the legion swine's.

Lucifer's son is born in secret.

The more filth the stronger Lucifer get.

The Holy and spiritual the people and honesty in prayer and worship gives God Hosanna supreme peace.

The essence of creation is humanity. Humanity is essentially God's heart.

The Supreme Thought God.

What is God's chalice?

How does God prepare for warfare?

Is God a might warrior?

Has God ever been defeated in war?

Gods first defeat:

The fall of the first angel in Heaven Lucifer he left with too much information on the kingdom, perhaps in blind sight hindsight God never saw this betrayal coming.

What is Gods arsnary?

As far as history tells as the source of Heavens head aches is one.

Code name Blasphemy and a swine and legions.

Yet on the kingdom of earth.

Behold there cometh the son of man.

Son of God Jesus Christ.

The Jesus - Judas effect.

It was written the betrayal and prophesied. God the kingdom and the angels were eternally prepared after the God - Debacle.

The Final Days Leading To Judgement Day.

The birth of the Luciferian Child named

Idol.

We won't indulge into the oaths.

Human sacrifices. Blood tithes. Not to undermine the Luciferians they really not that smart.

They flip everything upside down.

Turn a circle around it is still a circle.

Turn a triangle upside down it is still a triangle.

The key is to know your bible.

Beware of what dwells in your heart.

Have utter control of what enters your mind. Regulate thought. Let nothing out that will tarnish your reputation.

Judgement Day:

Is the day the spirit lives eternally in Heaven. God forbid the spirit dies and burns in Hell for eternity.

For the sake of creation God and Lucifer not face come face to face at least in the interim.

500 000 BC GC

Idol and Thought

Luciferian and God Child come face to face.

Till then Brethren keep the faith.

Lucifer cometh like a thief in the night.

Not to steal but to kill and destroy.

Invest not in God which rusts and is eaten by moth. Keep your salvation safe with God our Lord Jesus Christ.

Ok the year 500 000 BC GC

3 days before the 17th of August.

Thought had a dream. In his eyes he was being visited by an alien.

Thought was near a river it was flowing and calm. The strange creature human features yet rather lean and average height.

He called him by his name in the dream.

The God Child did not reply.

He called him the second time.

He responded how do you know my name. He could not utter a word he could not lie.

The 3rd time he called his same he was drawn to him like a magnet.

He used his magnetic field to naturally repel.

God sensed the God Child was in troubled. Asked the Guardians at the Palace in Houghton South Africa where the was. He is fast asleep dreaming father. He was now the age 33 you can imagine why God was anxious.

The alien seemed weak.

Yet when the enemy seems well he is strong. When is he perceived as far he is close. The Art of War.

When Thought was close enough to touch at arms length idol the Luciferian took 3 deep breaths they smelt like death

The forth breath swallowed a part of me they he crackled hackled laughed and vanished its as though he took my soul.

Come down thought Lucifer has no children the only person that could do that is Lucifer's Son.

I try reach heaven's land line telepathically, I dial the pager line, I Dad's cellular no network WTF that's an alarm God hears Thought God Childs distress and sends guardians to aid my distress.

A journey that would have taken 3 hours.

Took 18 hours.

Tonight God is on earth Houghton Estate.

Security is so tight it's underground.

There is not a fly on the wall.

The dogs are not allowed to bark.

After examining the event.

The elders deliberate.

Thought the God Childs soul, spirit and conscious has been snatched by an unknown entity highly unlikely.

When God head was born he had no Luciferian Child. That was the last time he was allowed on earth in ound unchained from 1000 mile bottomless and void pit to cause havoc and mislead the weak in faith only for a little while because only him and God know the day of judgement.

The elder on of elder screams

Oh My God.

God replies as in the EMOJI OMG

No Father.

Remember the night Thought the God Child it as born and we came to earth.

Lucifer was having a party. Yes sex drugs alcohol nothing there.

This party took place in Ethiopia

there were princess and goddess Caucasian and African.

God who you think one of the Goddess was Sheba

Queen Sheba

God replies to the Elders

OMG

The elders respond

As in Oh My God

God says no the EMOJI

OMG

What is the highest level of consciousness thought can reach?

Well let us have a look at the spectrum of thought. The highest thought is being closeness (oneness) with God.

Closeness (oneness) with God what does that really mean? The death of the ego. To let go of the self. A daily renewal through prayer mediation reading the Bible repenting and not sinning again as far as possible.

Most importantly keeping an eye on your salvation.

States of consciousness:

Innovative and creating something from nothing, alchemy. Building sectors of academia engineering building roads and bridges. Science and technology Artificial Intelligence advances in medicine health care and education.

Imagination manifesting from mind to matter, reality. Creativity the arts drama sports movies documentaries acting.

Creatives.

Pressures of survival:

Depression clinical sadness can lead to suicide.

The Prism of Consciousness.

The 2 magnetic fields which breath energy to life exhaling consciousness.

Primarily darkness and light
are the 2 magnetic forces in nature
which creation abides from.
Light and darkness are in equilibrium.

There was neither day or night in the beginning. Existence was void.

Time was yet to tick.

Time and life were yet to cross paths.

The sun light existed before the first moon rose. The light blinds the darkness.

Consciousness awareness awakens from this state. Day and night were born.

Till this day more then 3 billion years since day and night danced at dawn.

The moment.

The present.

The now is all we really have.

Tomorrow is a concept of worry.

Tomorrow is an ideology of anxiety.

If we pay due diligence to the present.

There is no need to be anxious about the future. Tomorrow consumed todays energy. Be present today.

If you focus on too much tomorrow fear creeps in you next few moves may be sloppy now tomorrow is suspect.

Just as the mind exists independent jof consciousness. The earth and water are the primarily the darkness and light of planet earth.

We have established in order for the process of reproduction process to take place. For procreation, intimacy for a child to be born

for the spirit to be conceived there to be a same species a male force and a female force.

Thus the sperm can germinate with the Ovary and the process of procreation manifests.

The moment of climax between man and woman is probably the most out of world experience amid sensation to the release of endorphins adrenaline and other hormones. Yet sex naturally without stimulants after the age of 40. Yet this is not cast in stone this vary from individual to individual.

Climatology what is the sensation when the weather is hot when the weather is hot what sensation you get?

Some people are depressed when the weather is hot .

Some people are happy when the weather is cold.

What you see as pretty may be unattractive to me.

What you fear may be my fetish.

In retrospect life is relative yet resolute and constant, change is a variable that is in equilibrium.

Human behaviour modification.

Variables human beings are born with a soul which harbours the spirit and your host is the human body.

You are given an identity at birth.

You are classified a boy or girl.

You are either male or female.

The male will fend for the family.

The female is fertile and will give birth to the children.

Humanity has followed this prototype for at least the past 6 000 years.

There have been religious wars.

There have been masses of mass distraction. Migrants, Xenophobia, Tsunamis, Forest fires, Ozone Layer Breaches, Cultural Supremacy.

Now the human mind is perverted the is human trafficking we are on the brinks of moral extinction Sodom and Gomorrah all over again. Mankind with all this intelligence when will we ever learn.

What are your top 5 inventions that propelled humanity to the next dimension since the beginning of time.

1. The wheel.

2. The clock.

3. Pen and paper.

4. The internet GPS.

5. The motor car transport.

What are top 5 ingredients to mankind's downfall:

1. Racism.

2. Sin.

3.Lack of Remorse.

4. Repentance and Forgiveness is exhiled.

5. Man does not believe in himself how can he believe in God?

Thought is propelled to higher levels of consciousness by analysis and observation of one's behaviours.

Are you aware of the thoughts you keep?

What is the nature of your thought?

Do you believe in virtue?

Are you living for the day?

Facing the unpleasant inevitables.

What matters the most to you?

Inevitably adversity will snatch the grasp of your palm from it how does that reality make you feel?

Can thought reason beyond the confines of consciousness?

What is consciousness?

Energy confined within a space a prism called the mind. Within the mind lies segments of which consciousness will be streamlined and divided into sectors of thoughts instincts desires.

From consciousness we have dreams polar effect nightmares. Delicts of thought Alzheimer's and issues and the stigma of mental health.

So have established consciousness is independent of the mind. Yet they co exist for the organism to function and survive in reality.

Consciousness is biological..

Stress is mechanical a product of survival habitually there is famine in the land and animal or mankind can not pay the bond he just lost his job.

Stress is natural.

Stress is a force of nature.

Stress is neural primary at a glance neither positive or negative.

Yet stress unexamined can collapse the entire nervous system without an army and a coup. Stress is the dangerous by any imaginable extreme.

Pay close attention to the events in your life that may stress you. Study your mistakes that is the indigenous way to grow and turn tragedy to lessons.

Pressure is a force exerted internally.

Pressure is a force exerted externally.

Pressure is a for at the core of the organism biologically and intellectually.

Your inability to cope with pressure.

Your coping skills of pressure determine weather you will survive.

The underline the truth if the matter weather you will surpass the maindaine and great like those that came before you your ancestors.

What are the barriers to the development of thought? What enhances the advances of the ideology of thought propergating intellectual stimuli.

Primary 9 Fields of thought:

Acadmia.

Sports.

Politics.

Religion.

Criminology

The Judetary.

The Prison System and

Health care system.

The education system.

What is the highest level of consciousness thought can reach?

Well let us have a look at the spectrum of thought. The highest thought is being closeness (oneness) with God.

Closeness (oneness) with God what does that really mean? The death of the ego. To let go of the self. A daily renewal through prayer mediation reading the Bible repenting and not sinning again as far as possible.

Most importantly keeping an eye on your salvation.

States of consciousness:

Innovative and creating something from nothing, alchemy. Building sectors of academia engineering building roads and bridges. Science and technology Artificial Intelligence advances in medicine health care and education.

Imagination manifesting from mind to matter, reality. Creativity the arts drama sports movies documentaries acting.

Creatives.

Pressures of survival:

Depression clinical saddness can lead to suicide.

...

The Prism of Consciousness.

The 2 magnetic fields which breath energy to life exhaling consciousness.

Primarily darkness and light

are the 2 magnetic forces in nature

which creation abides from.

Light and darkness are in equilibrium.

There was neither day or night in the beginning. Existence was void.

Time was yet to tick.

Time and life were yet to cross paths.

The sun light existed before the first moon rose. The light blinds the darkness.

Consciousness awareness awakens from this state. Day and night were born.

Till this day more then 3 billion years since day and night danced at dawn.

The moment.

The present.

The now is all we really have.

Tomorrow is a concept of worry.

Tomorrow is an ideology of anxiety.

If we pay due diligence to the present.

There is no need to be anxious about the future. Tomorrow consumed todays energy. Be present today.

If you focus on too much tomorrow fear creeps in you next few moves may be sloppy now tomorrow is suspect.

Just as the mind exists independent of consciousness. The earth and water are the primarily the darkness and light of planet earth.

We have established in order for the process of reproduction process to take place. For procreation, intimacy for a child to be born

for the spirit to be concieved there to be a same species a male force and a female force.

Thus the sperm can germinate with the Overy and the process of procreation manifests.

The moment of climax between man and woman is probably the most out of world experience amd sensation to the release of endorphins adrenaline and other hormones. Yet sex naturally without stimulants after the age of 40. Yet this is not cast in stone this vary from individual to individual.

Climatology what is the sensation when the weather is hot when the weather is hot what sensation you get?

Some people are depressed when the weather is hot .

Some people are happy when the weather is cold.

What you see as pretty may be unattractive to me.

What you fear may be my fetish.

In retrospect life is relative yet resolute and constant, change is a variable that is in equilibrium.

Human behaviour modification.

Variables human beings are born with a soul which harbours the spirit and your host is the human body.

You are given an identity at birth.

You are classified a boy or girl.

You are either male or female.

The male will fend for the family.

The female is fertile and will give birth to the children.

Humanity has followed this prototype for at least the past 6 000 years.

There have been religious wars.

There have been masses of mass distraction. Migrants, Xenaphobia, Tsunamis, Forest fires, Ozone Layer Breaches, Cultural Supremacy.

Now the human mind is perverted the is human trafficking we are on the brinks of moral extinction Sodom and Gomorrah all over again. Mankind with all this intelligence when will we ever learn.

What are your top 5 inventions that propelled humanity to the next dimension since the beginning of time.

1. The wheel.
2. The clock.
3. Pen and paper.
4. The internet GPS.
5. The motor car transport.

What are top 5 ingredients to mankind's downfall:

1. Racism.
2. Sin.
3.Lack of Remorse.
4. Repentance and Forgiveness is exhiled.
5. Man does not believe in himself how can he believe in God?

Thought is propelled to higher levels of consciousness by analysis and observation of one's behaviours.

Are you aware of the thoughts you keep?

What is the nature of your thought?

Do you believe in virtue?

Are you living for the day?

Facing the unpleasant inevitables.

What matters the most to you?

Inevitably adversity will snatch the grasp of your palm from it how does that reality make you feel?

Can thought reason beyond the confinds of consciousness?

What is consciousness?

Energy confined within a space a prism called the mind. Within the mind lies segments of which consciousness will be streamlined and divided into sectors of thoughts instincts desires.

From consciousness we have dreams polar effect nightmares. Delicts of thought Alzheimer's and issues and the stigma of mental health.

So have established consciousness is independent of the mind. Yet they co exist for the organism to function and survive in reality.

Consciousness is biological..

Stress is mechanical a product of survival habitually there is famine in the land and animal or mankind can not pay the bond he just lost his job.

Stress is natural.

Stress is a force of nature.

Stress is neural primary at a glance neither positive or negative.

Yet stress unexamined can collapse the entire nervous system without an army and a coup. Stress is the dangerous by any imaginable extreme.

Pay close attention to the events in your life that may stress you. Study your mistakes that is the indigenous way to grow and turn tragedy to lessons.

Pressure is a force exerted internally.

Pressure is a force exerted externally.

Pressure is a for at the core of the organism biologically and intellectually.

Your inability to cope with pressure.

Your coping skills of pressure determine weather you will survive.

The underline the truth if the matter weather you will surpass the maindaine and great like those that came before you your ancestors.

What are the barriers to the development of thought? What enhances the advances of the ideology of thought propergating intellectual stimuli.

Primary 9 Fields of thought:

Acadmia.

Sports.

Politics.

Religion.

Criminology

The Judetary.

The Prison System and

Health care system.

The education system.

What is the highest level of consciousness thought can reach?

Well let us have a look at the spectrum of thought. The highest thought is being closeness (oneness) with God.

Closeness (oneness) with God what does that really mean? The death of the ego. To let go of the self. A daily renewal through prayer mediation reading the Bible repenting and not sinning again as far as possible.

Most importantly keeping an eye on your salvation.

States of consciousness:

Innovative and creating something from nothing, alchemy. Building sectors of academia engineering building roads and bridges. Science and technology Artificial Intelligence advances in medicine health care and education.

Imagination manifesting from mind to matter, reality. Creativity the arts drama sports movies documentaries acting.

Creatives.

Pressures of survival:

Depression clinical sadness can lead to suicide.

...

The Prism of Consciousness.

The 2 magnetic fields which breath energy to life exhaling consciousness.

Primarily darkness and light

are the 2 magnetic forces in nature

which creation abides from.

Light and darkness are in equilibrium.

There was neither day or night in the beginning. Existence was void.

Time was yet to tick.

Time and life were yet to cross paths.

The sun light existed before the first moon rose. The light blinds the darkness.

Consciousness awareness awakens from this state. Day and night were born.

Till this day more then 3 billion years since day and night danced at dawn.

The moment.

The present.

The now is all we really have.

Tomorrow is a concept of worry.

Tomorrow is an ideology of anxiety.

If we pay due diligence to the present.

There is no need to be anxious about the future. Tomorrow consumed todays energy. Be present today.

If you focus on too much tomorrow fear creeps in you next few moves may be sloppy now tomorrow is suspect.

Just as the mind exists independent of consciousness. The earth and water are the primarily the darkness and light of planet earth.

We have established in order for the process of reproduction process to take place. For procreation, intimacy for a child to be born

for the spirit to be concieved there to be a same species a male force and a female force.

Thus the sperm can germinate with the Overy and the process of procreation manifests.

The moment of climax between man and woman is probably the most out of world experience amd sensation to the release of endorphins adrenaline and other hormones. Yet sex naturally without stimulants after the age of 40. Yet this is not cast in stone this vary from individual to individual.

Climatology what is the sensation when the weather is hot when the weather is hot what sensation you get?

Some people are depressed when the weather is hot .

Some people are happy when the weather is cold.

What you see as pretty may be unattractive to me.

What you fear may be my fetish.

In retrospect life is relative yet resolute and constant, change is a variable that is in equilibrium.

Human behaviour modification.

Variables human beings are born with a soul which harbours the spirit and your host is the human body.

You are given an identity at birth.

You are classified a boy or girl.

You are either male or female.

The male will fend for the family.

The female is fertile and will give birth to the children.

Humanity has followed this prototype for at least the past 6 000 years.

There have been religious wars.

There have been masses of mass distraction. Migrants, Xenaphobia, Tsunamis, Forest fires, Ozone Layer Breaches, Cultural Supremacy.

Now the human mind is perverted the is human trafficking we are on the brinks of moral extinction Sodom and Gomorrah all over again. Mankind with all this intelligence when will we ever learn.

What are your top 5 inventions that propelled humanity to the next dimension since the beginning of time.

1. The wheel.

2. The clock.

3. Pen and paper.

4. The internet GPS.

5. The motor car transport.

What are top 5 ingredients to mankind's downfall:

1. Racism.

2. Sin.

3.Lack of Remorse.

4. Repentance and Forgiveness is exhiled.

5. Man does not believe in himself how can he believe in God?

Thought is propelled to higher levels of consciousness by analysis and observation of one's behaviours.

Are you aware of the thoughts you keep?

What is the nature of your thought?

Do you believe in virtue?

Are you living for the day?

Facing the unpleasant inevitables.

What matters the most to you?

Inevitably adversity will snatch the grasp of your palm from it how does that reality make you feel?

Can thought reason beyond the confines of consciousness?

What is consciousness?

Energy confined within a space a prism called the mind. Within the mind lies segments of which consciousness will be streamlined and divided into sectors of thoughts instincts desires.

From consciousness we have dreams polar effect nightmares. Delicts of thought Alzheimer's and issues and the stigma of mental health.

So have established consciousness is independent of the mind. Yet they co exist for the organism to function and survive in reality.

Consciousness is biological..

Stress is mechanical a product of survival habitually there is famine in the land and animal or mankind can not pay the bond he just lost his job.

Stress is natural.

Stress is a force of nature.

Stress is neural primary at a glance neither positive or negative.

Yet stress unexamined can collapse the entire nervous system without an army and a coup. Stress is the dangerous by any imaginable extreme.

Pay close attention to the events in your life that may stress you. Study your mistakes that is the indigenous way to grow and turn tragedy to lessons.

Pressure is a force exerted internally.

Pressure is a force exerted externally.

Pressure is a for at the core of the organism biologically and intellectually.

Your inability to cope with pressure.

Your coping skills of pressure determine weather you will survive.

The underline the truth if the matter weather you will surpass the maindaine and great like those that came before you your ancestors.

What are the barriers to the development of thought? What enhances the advances of the ideology of thought propergating intellectual stimuli.

Primary 9 Fields of thought:

Academia.

Sports.

Politics.

Religion.

Criminology

The Judetary.

The Prison System and

Health care system.

The education system.

Thought Sent A Tweet To God Raising Hell Amongst The Arch Angels:

(The Birth of The God Child).

What If Love Was Never Betrayed

Would jealousy have seen the day of light?

What if the eye never wondered

in a moment of breaking our continent.

The art of prayer.

The subtle choice of commitment.

The disciple.

The sacrifice and staying committed when it was not fashionable.

What is the language of the gods?

What is the language of the dead?

What would we find inside gods mind?

What is the currency of the gods?

What is the currency of the dead?

What are the struggles of the dead?

What are the struggles of the dead?

Life is a reflection of eternity.

Fear yesterday today is trapped in its choices.

Tomorrow is a prisoner of the past.

The is buried alive it is dying to come life.

What could tomorrow hold for us?

Awaken tomorrow today what is it that see?

The beast has a child where there is power there is a source of nourishing.

Man duplicated ideas only to make the mind dull and degenerate.

Thought is sensitive protect its authenticity.

Who is your god would you ever betray him?

Doubt is a fire.

Love is forest of hope.

Don't let doubt burn down the potential of your dreams coming to life.

Keep your dreams alive by any means necessary. The burning dream.

The dying dream. The broke dream.

The dream that has not been beyond the boundaries of the mind. The dream living in reality. The dream that has a touch of the future.

Have you seen the pity of the dream that is blinded by yesterday. Yesterday was once filled with potential and hope. Yet I squandered my inheritance. Now I can not help but live in the past. I am living yet I am a figment of history.

Look into my eyes what is it that you see?

A nightmare stalks the mind unconsciously.

Your primary dream is dying to come to life.

The pressures of survival drive the mind crazy.

Can you think under pressure?

How do you cope with intense levels of stress?

Have you studied the stimulates of stress in your life? What triggers you?

What breaks your heart?

What worry's your mind?

Is it well with your soul?

There are some simple questions.

What is the state of your finances?

Are you living comfortably?

Are you living from hand to mouth?

These 2 questions will determine is you are prone to be controlled, manipulated and abused physically, psychologically and emotionally.

Are your primary relationships healthy?

Are mum and dad supportive of your dreams?

Are your sibling pursuing and manifesting their dreams in reality?

The reflection of the childhood of the man.

A glimpse of the heart of the woman.

Are you a loving, supportive partner?

Is your spouse complementary and faithful in her way that is a treasure a jewel which never dies even after death.

What is your perception of god?

What shaped your relationship with God?

What are your views on faith?

What would you cast out your mind?

What is holding you back from manifesting you inner most desires?

Are living to die?

If not are we molding and shaping our destiny through our reality today.

What are your strengths do they outweigh your weaknesses?

God is the king thought.

Yet a negative thought seeks to displace the kingdom of the almighty God.

Thought is the product of time.

Analysis, observing and studying behaviour and natural particles and their isotopes.

The psychology of existence.

The relevance of yesterday.

The hardships of today.

The demeanour of tomorrow the unknown.

What is the meaning of life?

What if God died a natural death the day the Garden Eden fell. This would have caused pain of amongst mankind yet to inhabit the planet earth.

What if the devil died a natural death?

Would darkness cease to exist?

Would that be the end of all negative thought?

Would the mind be restored to virtue?

Would the world be made a better place?

What if the mind died a natural death?

What is consciousness died a natural death ?

What if love was never betrayed?

The Keys To The idle Mind:
The door to the heart.
The safe which houses the convent of the soul.
The art of prayer is vital.
Yet the shadow is the presence of your ancestors and God closer then you can ever imagine.
Who holds the keys to an idle mind?
What are your dreams?
What are your aspirations?
What are your circumstances?
What are your fears?
What jewels live in your reality?
What are your treasures?
The Christened thought.
The haunted consciousness.
The living ghost.
The suspicious human beings.
Terrified they are marked for death
by a ghost.
The bestowed intentions
The relics of our past:
Vintage memories which weigh on our present reality we can not run from our shadow as long as we live.
The contemporary thought:
Classic.
A golden era.
A moment of brilliance.
At a glance society, culture and human race will be shaped for centuries to come, all in the name of the light bulb, technology and inventions.
The complacent motive:
Once aligned with thought.

The motive could have gone to over power the thought.

Yet the motive did not seek power.

What is the price of peace? What is the stance of war?

The manifesting dream:

The thought.

The motive.

Breed in the mind for decades.

Moulded & sculptured into the ideal thought.

Watch them as they leave the mind.

There is nothing as beautiful as a manifesting dream in reality. What is the potential of the dream once it has manifested in reality?

What is the lifecycle of the dream?

Does the dream live beyond the lifespan of the human being? The dream can die as a concept in the mind. The dream can die as a living dream in reality.

The suspicious neighbour

This human being is shady.

He is not to be trusted.

What is it about him.

His body language.

His smirk.

The glare in his eyes.

What are we going to do move out?

Only to move into a estate with some rich kids with new money we were once one of them.

We could move into an farm estate.

We have nice problems.

I know dear life has been resourceful and full of splendour and surprise.

The broken mind.

The bent thought.

The living sleep.

The sceptic decision not sure weather what is right is wrong either what's wrong is right?

The intricacies process of thinking:

Mending a broken mind.

Examining the content of the mind.

Changing thought to bring to life the ideology

of my existence.

If not manifesting dreams

what else are we living for?

Go ahead take the keys of the idle mind:

What are yodecades.through of thought are our deeds.

The shadows of thought are our motives.

Thoughts themselves are a reflection of our consciousness an image of the mind a spectrum of what lies in our hearts.

Consciousness is the content of our very existence. Our consciousness is parallel to existence. Our imagination is our spiritual fingerprint.

What separates man from his neighbour is his thoughts.

Where do thoughts come thoughts.

How do thoughts get embedded into our consciousness?

Intra thoughts:

Thoughts that are born in the mind.

Extra thoughts:

External thoughts.

Thoughts which have an external influence.

Intra domestic thoughts.

Thoughts that leave the mind physically as psychological dreams and influence reality.

Extra international thoughts.

Thoughts that already live in reality shaping society in the now moulding ideologies and future concepts and thoughts yet to be born.

The sausery perhaps mystery of thought.

Some thoughts walk on fire.

Some thoughts turn water into ice, fridges.

Some thoughts gathered over centuries built bridges roads connect towns cities are aligned.

On a fundermental level mankind is nolonger concerned with misery suffering and ear. Mankind is building spaceship galaxyships and voygering into unchartered lands, outer space.

Yet in reality the world is broken.

The crack pipe is burning.

The pimps on the corner.

The hoes on the pole at the strip stacking pennies to oay for her university tuition let alone reality that rent has not been paid in 3 months.

Humànity is in trouble.

All the wisdom in the world.

Curiosity killed a cat.

Who will save you?

Who will save me?

When you are depleted on empty.

When you have no reserves.

Do you turn to self is that not vanity?

Leaning on your own understanding.

The devil is in the back seat of your consciousness and you feeling vulnerable and edgy call on God Jesus Christ.

Amen and Amen.

What is the function of dreams?

Are dreams superficial on a basic level?

Are dreams hereditary on a spiritual level?

Dreams have a destiny.

Do dreams have fears?

Dreams are a collection of thoughts.

Dreams are a refined ideology.

Dreams are reposed desires dying to come alive.

Dreams transgress the boarders of time space and matter. Dreams are not governed by gravity and time.

Do dreams fall in line with reality?

Do some dreams hate reality?

Do some dreams breathe?

Do some dreams die in the mind?

Do some dreams die an unnatural death?

Do some dreams suffocate before they become thoughts?

What is the distinction between a dream and a thought again I ask?

What is the frequency which a dream operates?

Is a dream fixed?

Is a dream bilingual?

Do dreams communicate with one another?

Do dreams communicate with thought?

Are dreams born maternally?

Do dreams communicate with the heart?

What are the type of dreams?

Some dreams are in plain sight.

Some dreams are hidden from the author the mind.

Some dreams are stumbled upon.

Some dreams are imposed upon us by society and our elders.

What happens to the dreams that die in the mind? Are they recycled into new dreams?

What is the source of dreams?

Do all dreams come from one place? The race against time is to grasp the lessons and master circumstances manifestation of dreams while time breathes along your shadow.

A dream that is forming.

What is the physical appearance of a dream? Is a dream conceived in the mind?

What is the state of the dream before it is born?

On the conception of the dream.

How many dreams are needed for a new dream to be born.

How much time is needed for a new dream to form in the mind?

How much time is needed for a dream to form in reality is relative.

In the mind a dream lives the life span of the organism.

In reality the dream can live for centuries.

Metaphysics

What lies within the boundaries of the mind?

What exists outside the boarders of the mind?

The elements of the imagination.

What is the image of consciousness?

What is the image of the sub consciousness? What is the image of the unconscious?

What is the image of thought?

What is the image of energy?

What is the image of the dream?

What is the image of the nightmare primarily?

Is the image independent of the projectory?

What is the image?

How does the image form?

Where does the image live?

Where do images come from?

What is the process for the image to manifest in reality?

It is a metaphysis for the image to convert into a thought.

Can you tell the difference between a

Image

Thought

Vision

Dream

Nightmare

Ideology

Philosophy

Doctrine

Energy is primarily the basis for the transfiguration of life.

Consciousness is the mirror of the ego psyche and persona of the mind.

The process of thinking.

As a man thinketh.

How much energy goes into compiling 2 thoughts. How much energy goes into compiling an abstract ideology?

What is the function of thought?

Beyond thinking what is the ideology of thought.

What is the purpose of dreams?

Dream.

Let Us Take A Closer Look.

At The Greatest illusion Mankind Pulled Over The Masses. Does Money Exist On A Fundamental Level? Part 2 of 2

Numbering.

Biblical times.

The census.

Monitoring every living human soul.

Arius measuring of tracking the movement and communication of all human beings across all classes races and status.

The birth certificate is arguably one of the important documents that the government will ever own of you in your existence in this lifetime.

What does the birth

Certificate tell us about you?

The month, date, year you were born.

Your gender, race and ethnicity.

Your name and surname is your birth c3rrificate. As well as the ID number of your biological mother amd father on an abridged birth certificate.

All this classified information on a single A4 document. That is power. That is dangerous. The federal government of every nation has all this public yet classifi3r information.

Your bank account is your next most important asset while you live.

What do you keep in your bank account your money. Your inheritance.

You work hard for your money.

You work your entire lifetime for your money and you keep it In a bank account.

You buy land and keep your estates and businesses in trusts so if your children are learned they can pass down the skill from generation to generation.

Yet things do not always go as PLANNED.

Death is sudden unexpected and unplanned. If your seedlings are childlike at a mature age over age the kingdom no matter how mighty no matter how much resources the kingdom will fall with a single lifetime what tool 400 years to accumulate.

Can money buy you wisdom Funder mentally?

Can money buy you understanding?

Circumstances.

Can money buy you love?

Can money buy you sleep?

Can money buy you peace?

Money will buy you debt.

Money will buy land.

Money will buy you the car of your dreams.

Money will pay off your off your dream home and wedding.

Money will send your children to primary school.

In the material world money will buy you every thing under the sun.

Can money buy you time?

Can money buy you happiness?

Can money buy you salvation?

Can money buy a place in heaven?

Will money buy you love?

What is the place of the value of money in your life?

Today is alive.

Breathe.

3 trillion sperm God and the universe choose you. You special you a dream come true. You a manifestation of reality.

From mind to matter.

The metaphysical the spirit and the shadow learn in the realm of the physical no one really I understands the intention of motive. What is the purpose of thought?

Where is humanity headed.

What does it mean to be alive?

8 billion thoughts at the same place inhabiting the perimeter of planet earth.

Thoughts are cut of the same fabric.

Ultimately separated by distance, time and space.

What is time?

The measurement of the ages.

Seasons.

Climatology.

Eons, centuries and decades.

Years, months, weeks, days, hours and seconds.

Space:

The distance between 2 objects.

The objects are either stagnent.

The objects are either moving towards each other drawn by a magnetic field.

The objects are either mover away from each other repelled by a magnetic field.

Distance:

The time and space it takes to move from one place to another.

The variable of distance is velocity mass and space.

Mass:

Weight.

A physical object a constant which is a living organism cold blooded or warm blooded. Or a stationary object like a mountain rock mountain or ocean.

Thought:

Transcends boundaries of 3xistance.

Mind over matter to reality.

Thought is the image of the mind.

Thought is the perception of the heart.

Thought is am element of the imagination.

Breath:

Is the distance between life and death.

Heaven:

Heaven is adjact to what lies in a human beings mind which ultimately will reveal what is hidden in the mind.

Hell:

Is a heart which is repelling all projections of light. Oppresses the meek. Instigates terror on peace and sabotages the plans God has for his chosen people.

Perhaps hell only exists on earth.

The Nature of The Heart

The heart is more then an organ is that true? Could the heart be the alter the convenient between the flesh and the spirit. Flesh of my flesh. Blood of my blood.

The nature of the heart is bare.

Naked.

Sinful.

Secretive.

Contagious.

Cunning and ambiguous.

Dexterous to say the least.

The heart conceals motive.

What is the storage capacity of the brain?

How much thought can the mind process? How many thoughts can the heart process per minutes?

The brain.

The mind.

The heart.

Consciousness.

The unconsciousness.

Motive.

As a man thinketh the sub conscious mind is born.

For who knows for sure what the heart thinketh?

Words are laced with venom.

Flattery will charm a damsel.

Fear is disguised as a missionary

by the time you understand the essence of the Holy book your mind has been decolonised.

Knowledge is a double edged sword.

The most skillful warrior will succeed at the combact of war. Remember if not peace what are you Fighting for?

Could the purpose of the heart be to disrupt the quest for peace in one's mind? Is motive the army. The treachery of darkness will not rest till shadows rule the flesh.

What is the purpose of thought?

What is the cause?

What is the chemical reaction that caused a negative thought and positive Thoughts to form a segment of thought known as motive.

Is motive independent of thinking?

Motive branches from thought forming a sub sector of thought known as the sub conscious mind.

What is the content of a negative thought? Ultimately these will be the constitutes of a negative mind.

The Utterance of Truth Is Unspoken:

Deaf

Numb.

Actions speak louder then words so they say my Lord.

The tongue is wild by nature, it can not be tamed. The tongue conceal the agenda of the heart. Not many have been able to apprehend their tongue in the vegar of their youth thus thy are slave to the desires of their passions.

The truth is the sun.

The birth give birth to life.

Yet the truth I unexamied and understood can blind you instantly while innocently gazing at the facts.

Upon judgement of virtue there are no witnesses the solitude of innocence is upon solitude alone desolate sober and what to advance the propaganda of the fate of destiny.

Lies are restless.

Quick to anger.

Temperas.

Venomous.

Lies will strike without heed.

What are the attributes of a positive thought?

What is the content of a positive thought? Where is thought headed? What is the reference point when one's begins to understand the psychology of motive?

The truth is neither a negative thought.

The truth does not broadcast a positive thought. The truth is a projection of consciousness from the mind into reality.

The continents in reality are variables fixed stationary and moveable. Life is alive death breathes from the womb of the under belly of the abyss of the underworld.

Thought is born in the mind.

Motive is a fruit of thought.

Yet motive begat consciousness and outmuscled thought.

No one knows the seat of motive.

How did motive come into existence?

What sparked motive to take its first breath. First step. God forbid its first thought?

Are thought and motive primarily one?

Where is thought headed?

Where is motive headed?

Where am I headed?

How long will I take me get my destination? Then I have arrived then what?

Perception paralysis
Astro Projection
Without Probable Cause
Animated Thoughts
Bridges of Deceit

The Nature of The Heart
Astro Projection
Without Probable Cause
Have You Ever Imagined Living In A Day Independent From The Measurement of The Instrument of Time?

.

Alliance of The Triangles:

When the stars align.

And the planets orbit in supreme precision the tim zones become obsolete.

Have you imagined living in a day independent of the measurement of the I student of time?

The belly of time is aging.

Yet time is alive.

Time is breathing.

Time is a spirit.

Time is a organ.

Yet time does not grow old.

Time does not rest.

Time has never been late in 3.5 billion years. Time must be a close acquaintance of God.

Time has never missed a moment in history. Time is present. Time shall meet the future it is even a concept let alone born.

What can rival time?

With life you create the moments time will remember.

Can you stretch your thoughts and expand your mind? Beyond the boundaries of the perception of reality. Consciousness is an elastic not made of plastic.

Death is a fatality.

Is it really ever game over once the soul has come into existence.

Breath is eternal.

Yet can thoughts be recycled?

Perhaps habits form character based on repetition and instinct. The natural drives of the human being.

Thought is divided by the consequences of choice. Thought is United by the execution of a well thought out plan till it's implementation & recommendations are well executed.

Insticts are raw emotions they are not easily tamed it takes a skillful soul to grasp the nature and depths of one's heart.

The mind is a temple.

Thought is the alter.

The action is the sacrifice.

The sin is the state of reality and society.

Are you living the manifestation of your dream. Do you know your purpose. What will you magnify with your gift of life?

What do the fruits of effort constitute?

Indigenous Vibes Retribution & Spiritual

Sclerosis.

Close Your Eyes Op n Your Mind:

Visualise tapping into the centre of your universe.

Centre yourself.

Let your light shine through.

Let's go deep within the being.

Let us breathe beyond the boundaries of existence.

What will we find beyond the boundaries of existence?

If there is life beyond the boundaries of existence.

Then we are still trapped within a sphere or realm of life? True of false?

Can there be existence without life?

What is life?

A force which carries energy releasing it on the oath on earth leading each spirit towards its destiny beyond our planet the fate of the spirit and soul will be unveiled according by your deeds and reputation.

Watch carefully the shadow follows observes and watches over you never judging nor condemning in your lifetime.

We are explorers by nature let us leave the flesh telekinesis we time travel astro projection we leave our earth leaving the body all have is our consciousness spirit and soul.

We find a bottomless pit void with no beginning with no ending in sight as far as the natural eye can see. Have we found an element of creation that exists already? Yes.

The question remains.

Is there a place below beneath besides the sun that does not exist? A place that has not been discovered. Beyond voygership is there a place within our universe galaxy that is yet to exist?

Yes, No & Perhaps Maybe Neither?

Is it possible for the soul to leave the flesh into a state of existence yet as a formless nothingness hollow stratosphere which still exists within a perimeter of a boarder some where, yet the location remains unverified on GPS.

Some places satellites can't reach yet.

Perhaps.

Yet the desired state remains when the soul leaves the body to ascend into Heaven. To be amongst God and the gods. The supreme thought ideology.

Inhale and exhale.

Get inside your breath.

Hold it.

Don't let go.

Don't breathe.

Don't inhale.

Don't exhale.

Let your breath carry your consciousness out of your body.

In this moment you are not bound to time. Your perception of reality is about to be transformed.

Your soul has left this body hovering over your body like a halo you are the presence of Greatness.

Gazing at your shadow. You are in the mists of a living angel. In this dream nothing is what it may seem.

Place close attention to your thoughts.

In retrospect release them empty your mind of the burdens of today. Yesterday carries the breath of tomorrow.

Before you let go of your motives.

Study them from a distance least they be on guard and catch you unalert.

The game of combact is brutal.

The only casualty is defeat.

Winner takes all.

Your weaknesses are paramount to your stumbles. Eliminate all broken chains in your circle leave no room for betrayal the Judas effect.

Indigenous Vibes Retribution & Spiritual
    Sclerosis
    A Poem By
    Nkosinathi 2Pistolz Ncala

Ima Set Consciousness On Fire.
I heard em say that the devil is a liar.
Where can I find truth?
I open and search my mind.
Guess what? I just find trash.
How do recycle the garage in my mind?
How did it get here in the first place?
Be weary of the thought you keep?
I stretch my thoughts I stumble across a motive.
Where can I find truth?
I open my heart.
It's riddled with secrets laced with venom
The tongue is a deadly weapon concealing the desires of the human being.

Beauty for who can resist one night with a Goddess? All the treasures in the world the super car the mansion in the grander scale beyond the mundane and existence.

Who's heart is safe in your hands and you are the reflection of her life in he eyes. That is the honey comb the crown jewel in the spiritual layer of motives no one quite knows what are their intentions they must be cold blooded they can't be trusted.

So I lean on my own understanding now I am even more confused.

They say make the most of the cards you were dealt. I analyse the game. I study the cards I was dealt. I do the math. I do not have a scathing chance in hell on leaving alive as for the concept of heaven.

The game of life is rigged.

You either rich or you poor.

Black or White.

Without money you can not buy a house car take your children to a good school get married insurance travel save and have more children.

As a male in life it's the domino effect.

You have 2 choices in life 2 roads.

The book (education) or the gun

(organised crime) Education will buy you freedom legally. The trigger the corner the pimp the hoe the pole.

Freedom is promised at birth yet how many acquire it in their lifetime?

Lets manifest our dreams on earth while there is still time.

I turn to the gospel.

Religions are war.

Perhaps that's the enemies plot.

Yet look deeper at the underlying source of the pain.

Put the illness diagnose aside for a second. Where does the arthritis bipolar cancer come from. What triggers the mutation of the cell?

Go beyond the root of the pain.

The medication will heal.

If you are psychologically prepared you will be the scab that speeds up the process.

A Poem By

Nkosinathi 2Pistolz Ncala

The Unblemished Thought

Today we have a peace offering.

We are in the presence of an Unblemished thought 89 years not a single known negative thought has transgressed this noble mind.

As these are the Unblemished thoughts last days on earth. We perform a celebration to Jehovah in jubilation that his offspring seedlings shall now carry the DNA and Genetics of the Unblemished thought to their children and their children's children.

Let us sacrifice a live dove.

Bring and let us lay it next to a dead dove. Bring flour for cake and the finest oil in the land.

The ceremony was concealed.

The guests were honours.

All attendees were sworn to secrecy.

The elder is no longer with us.

Yet the Unblemished thought is amongst us. It will surface in the mind that has no room for darkness. The meek compromise the mission to defeat the forces of darkness without waging war.

Have you ever tasted victory without any casualties it is so sweet.

The Unblemished Thought.

Now that thought has been cut from the umbilical cord of consciousness.

Thought is independent from the mind.

Thought is unbound to the confines of the pressures of survival.

What is the primary cause that causes thought to go astray from its destiny and fate? Money may seem to be the root of all problems at face value.

The question is how do you seek to attain your currency? How do you spend your salary? How many sources of income do you have? What are your needs? What are your wants? What is your ambition to magnify your sources of income?

There is absolutely nothing sinister with attaining and expanding your money capital base.

Money has no spirit. Money won't get you salvation. No one is taking their money to heaven. What matters is do you have enough money to last you this lifetime?

How much time will you need to attain this type of wealth? When you look at you dynasty how many generations would you like your family inheritance to regenerate 4 generations.

The Bible says a man has done well if his wealth lasts 4 generations 400 years your children's children will live in family homes mansions and palaces you and your wife envisioned and they magnify the wealth.

Yet you can build a nation without being the prime minister. You can form the ideologies of the manifesto of your ethics and code of virtue and moral conduct for your country of birth not single handily necessarily.

Your people shall govern the land and their , for 4 centuries 4 000 years.

Wealth is relative.

Success is mandatory.

Failure is not an option.

Suffering is cruelty against the constitution and the well being of the soul.

The Unblemished Thought

A Poem By
Nkosinathi Ncala

To Kneel Before Death.

I will not surrender my breath.

I will not bow to darkness.

I will not lean on my own understanding.

I will not be a slave to fear.

I will not render my salvation no matter how turbulent my circumstances may be perceived by my consciousness.

According to the Abrahamic convenent for your spirit and soul to rest in eternity your life force has to be summoned by Jehova.

Fear is the root of spiritual darkness. Depression is the seed of the force of darkness. Shame guilt envy jealousy greed are the fruits of a rotten consciousness. What can come from such a state of mind.

Without sin would there be death?

Who does sin submit to? Itself vanity.

Sin can not look reflection in the mirror.

Perhaps death would be natural unless by accidental cause.

Without sin would there be depression? highly unlikely. Would humanity be one nation? unlikely. Yet thought would be streamed in consciousness.

Without sin would there be crime murder rape? Highly unlikely those are stigmas of sin.

Without crime the mind would not live forever physically. Yet at least we would not be fighting these ignorant wars.

Perhaps a world without sin would bring us closer to the practical realisation of the concept of peace in one's living lifetime.

Sin is the manifestion of the perversion of thought within the mind projecting into the material world.

A Poem By

Nkosinathi 2Pistolz Ncala

Lift The Spirit Beyond ConsciousNESS

Through The Science of Breath:

Be still physically emotionally psychologically. Close your eyes what is it that you see?

Close your eyes till there is neither a reflection of darkness or light. The spectrum which reflects consciousness had been restricted from transmitting live images from the mind to the perception of consciousness.

Beyond your senses seeing hearing smell taste and touch the perception glands.

Cease the moment. You are temporarily free from the process of broadcasting images streaming consciousness.

Ladies and gentlemen coming live from somewhere in the mind no internet or data needed just thoughts of your choice you are at the station called the Liberation of Freedom.

Let us examine study and understand the mind its content and everything in it.

Why do we act the way we do? Why do we get aggressive when we are offended?

Why do we feel pain when we are hurt?

Why do we resist when we are in danger?

Why do we fall in love only to be betrayed?

You are living you alive yet you have no mind.

Your spirit has risen above you are in the presence of the Holy spirit.

Your life is your life.

You can't run from it unless you have made a mess of it.

Run, how far will you get?

Stop no matter how hopeless the situation tomorrow is another day it is going to be ok.

Now you have a bird's eye view of your problem. You have been granted a new perspective on Iife.

The ball is in your court.
Are you going for glory.
Will you play it safe and beg for mercy
when life does not proceed as planned.
Worry would not exist if yesterday's transgressions were resolved.
Do not let today escalate into tomorrow that is the seed of doubt.
What are you about?
How will those around you remember you? Did you impact your
community?
Will society remember you?

Lift The Spirit Beyond ConsciousNESS
    Through The Science of Breath:

A Poem By
    Nkosinathi 2Pistolz Ncala

What Does God Fear?

Above All Could It BE The Heart of ManKIND For Above All It Who Knows What Secrets It Hides.

How Can Love Conquer Fear?

History Judges The Living.
Today Is More Relevant Then Forever.

Lift The Spirit Beyond ConsciousNESS

If you look inside Gods mind independent of mankind s existence what would you find.

Heaven would exist.

The angels would be praising singing and worshipping. Lucifer Gabriel and Michael would still be the chief primary angels.

There would be harmony.

Hell was yet to be conceived.

The sun did it exist no.

The moon did it exist no.

The galaxy and planets did not exist.

There was no darkness.

There was no light.

There was life.

Time existed independent of gravity.

Death was yet to be born.

So does God exist in the flesh?

Are angels the soul?

The spirit could be the identity of the living being.

The sun moon day and night as in the book of genesis only formed after the forming of the garden of Eden.

Water is one of the first natural elements

God formed. Mankind shall not live off bread alone and the word was born.

So God gave Adam the first commandment do not eat off the tree of knowledge. For then you will be like the Gods you will be one of Us.

What is the tree of knowledge.

Spiritual cake.

The process of reproduction.

God told Adam you have the power of the tongue. Name every animal on the land the sea and Every fowl in the sky they are under your command.

Yet the Gods live forever they can not die a physical death.

Perhaps the commandment Lucifer transgressed was he ate from the tree of knowledge he interceded with of one Gods and Goddesses. What happened to the reign and bloodline of that child? That remains a mystery for the interim.

A Poem By

Nkosinathi 2Pistolz Ncala

Temptation of The Forsaken

Humanity if not peace what are we fighting for?

The God Child and Idol.

What will become of Gods chosen people? Jew or Gentile?

Who will lead Africa out of its poverty and suffering? When will hatred and racism collapse? We need a balanced way of life.

Survival is rigged. 1 percent are born into wealth. 99 percent are bruised on the heal. Essentially we are a species that comes from one womb. The infestation of confusion is that we do not share the same dream.

We are divided by our desire.

Our weaknesses are our own demise we are dying while we living. How does one lift the mind? How precious is your life to you?

What is the meaning of life?

Joy, pleasure and pain.

Suffering illness and agony.

The body is weak.

The mind is sick.

The spirit is empty.

How can I serve God when depression has a vice grip on my soul.

I have to find myself.

I can not give up now.

I had to remind myself.

Who will solve your problems?

If not you nobody.

Identify your problems.

Seek to understand your self firstly.

What drives you

Seek a wholestic view of your situation.

Where you at?

Where are you going?

How did you get here?

If you are stuck and in a jam.

How am I going to get out this mess I have created being the operative statement.

The Kingdom of Israel is at the mercy of time. Jerusalem is on its knees begging for mercy for the war with Palestine to draw to a cease fire.

Will the Jew and the Gentile Ever see eye to eye. Fighting our land boarders and the right to the Arch of God terrain will prevail.

Humanity if not Peace What Are We Fighting For?

A Poem By
Nkosinathi 2Pistolz Ncala

What Does God Fear?
Above All Could It BE The Heart of ManKIND For Above All It Who Knows What Secrets It Hides.

Humanity If Not Peace What Are We Fighting For?

History Judges The Living.
Today Is More Relevant Then Forever.

The Genealogy of Thought:

Thought Is One.

Yet thought has been divided by the rise of the ego. The fallacy of the self. The congruent of the centre.

Facets of fields of thought.

What do thoughts do on a daily basis.

They command the flesh.

Where the mind goes the body will follow. Monkey see monkey do.

We wake up.

While we are asleep could thought be united In a world of dreams. For some reason we have been conditioned to believe that our dreams belong to us solely.

Just as when we are conscious awake

we interact in a world called survival which a capitalist system. The world we live in. Is it benefiting our agenda?

Is the life you living daily aligned with your dreams? When all is said and done did you live a life worth remembering?

So thought primary is one.

Thought is the force which leads consciousness. Yet the content of consciousness is a variant intra independent of being flawless.

The jeopardy of choice is sin. What is wrong is wrong what is right is right.

Yet when the statement is made he

no longer has a conscious what does that really mean? Some of us are exempt from judgement. The scrutiny of today is the awakening of understanding.

Righteousness is seated on the throne of discernment.

Thoughts are born.

Thoughts are emotional they catch feelings. Thoughts are social beings.

Thoughts get lonely.

Thoughts get intelligent.

Yet some thoughts are dull.

Can thoughts distinguish between the world of reality dreams and nightmares?

What is the variation between thought and instinct.

What is the supreme thought.

God.

Omnipresent.

Everywhere.

At the same place at the same time.

At the same frequency and intensity.

God is independent of the force of life nude and death. In retrospect God is not regulated by the laws of gravity' and not bound to the constitution of any government God is the Law.

Remember the 10 commandments will lead through the darkness and command the darkness to give way to the light.

One day there will be no more darkness in the mind.

Who commands fear?

Who kneels towards righteousness?

Who can stand in the presence of an angel?

Who bows before God?

The Principles of Abundance - Make Up The Mind:
What do you fear?
Whom do you fear?
Why do they intimidate you?
Perhaps they used to love you?
Do you still love them?
Why do you stay in an unhappy relationship.
Perhaps you trapped.
Bad choices in life.

You have a single source not enough to get you and your child a better life. You can't afford to move out what would the neighbours say.

Remember you does not love you anymore. Pray meditate fast find a second job upskill child you will prevail victorious.

What makes you anxious?

You have to make a life changing choice why does doubt creep in in?

What is the difference between doubt, fear and anxiety.

Doubt:

Hesitate before you make a choice.

Fear:

Psychological primarily mind over matter playing games with the flesh.

Anxiety:

A combination of doubt and fear is has psychological and physical symptoms and release of hormones which with trauma which if unexamined trigger depression.

What do you envy?
What makes you jealous?
What makes you cry?
What makes you weak to your knows?

Are you more often. Vulnerable then you are in command.

Are you greedy?

Do you have money in abundance?

Do you have more then four sources of income one for everyday of the week?

At what age will you purchase your dream home? At what will you retire? And will age will you fulfil your prophecy?

When did you first have your primary dream? When will you manifest it into reality.

The principles of abundance remain constant.

The greater your effort is not independent of your geographical environment. The economic climate of the state and world bears a impact on the price of bread petrol rates levies and taxes.

The climate weather determines how much food the nation will harvest for the seasons. The rains effect our lives in ways I can not begin to phantom.

The principles of abundance.

Are not independent of your heart mind and emotional well being. Take nothing for granted in this life. Least it come back to haunt you.

The Principles of Abundance - Make Up Your Mind

A Poem By

Nkosinathi 2Pistolz Ncala

How Did The First Thought Manifest In The Human Mind?

Divine intervention?

Is thought man made?

Is thought a process of animals and species evolving?

What is the destiny of thought?

Is the fate of thought independent from the fate of man?

Creatures of creation give birth.

They nurture the young till they can fend for themselves. Yet humanity has evolved beyond the circumference of our natural habitat. Humanity has industrialised the concept of nature.

Currency has corrupted the nature of goodness. In 2024 the heart is ruled by greed, envy and jealousy the fall of virtue.

We need money to survive. In the modern society. The fact remains. After you have fought the battle called life when all is said and done money is not a natural resource.

So the establishment of the faculty of currency who is really benefiting? The expropriation of the natural resources of mother earth while the people of the land remain impoverished.

How long can the famine of poverty and suffering be allowed to stunt?

Why does life come to an end?

We are born to live out our dreams into reality.

Why do we have to die. The flesh grows old and meets its demise.

Flesh of my flesh. Ashes to ashes and dust to dust.

Bones will be consumed by maggots.

Mankind wants to live forever.

Mankind attained understanding.

Mankind's discernment transcended the boarders of the physical realm.

Mankind is an explorer.

Mankind transcends times zones.

Mankind builds space ships and transcends out of space.

Yet the some animal species which existed before mankind's rise are extinct if not on the endangered list. Our forests are being cut alarming rates so we can print more money so we can buy more furniture for homes and wood grain for our exotic cars.

The state of the ozone layer is a floor in our understanding of the importance of the balance of natural forces of nature. As well a bee is no less important then an ant.

Is man made purely of flesh.

Earth existence when the spirit can no longer carry the flesh.

Where does knowledge ascend from?

Yes wisdom is experience examination repetition and improving existing processes and systems.

So there is nothing beyond existence.

Reality is the pinnacle of existence.

Survival which is man made the 9 - 5

Is purely there to pay your bills. Comfort is a luxury are for the nobles. Poverty is a reality for the masses of the population.

Look around you nature was created by the force of existence the universe.

Without mankind the universe existence evolves and thrives without twitching or losing a limb.

Without the universe mankind would not even be a memory. Mankind would have have been given the opportunity to be adorned with a name and inherit a surname. Without nature mankind wouldn't be able to breath let alone to be born into the physical realm.

Mankind can not evolve without the universe. Mankind is conceived into nature. Thought manifests into the world of the natural elements wood, fire, water, air, gold, platinum, silver and gold.

A Poem By:

Nkosinathi 2Pistolz Ncala

Do Memories Live Forever?

Idols.

If they do?

What keeps memories alive for centuries after the flesh has been buried and your loved ones have forgotten to mourn.

The Gods need our prayers to sustain our faith hope and dreams. Once man worships forgein Gods Melton brazen Baal lot Moab Ammon the Gods get furious ad strike the earth with famine and tragedy.

Let the good woman.

Thy womb be shut and no prophet shall be born in God's land for 400 years.

Why do the Gods scorn idols with such rage, violence and abomination?

The human heart is God's alter.

Sin is unacceptable it causes chaos and confusion in the spiritual realm. Blasphemy is treason.

Phonication and adultery compromises vows which where taken before God. Till death do us part.

How is God to regulate sin?

The commandments are ideal yet God has given mankind free WILL.

By the time the sin is committed and it becomes a crime it is to late.

The jail's are with juveniles.

Death Row is inhuman.

A life for another will never solved our problems.

How are we to clean up our streets and make them safe again? Have you imparted & idealised an advanced community forum which would make society a safer place almost instantly?

Once you have witnessed a crime?

Once you have been abused physically emotionally psychologically financially controlled and manipulated. What impact does your abuse have on the way you perceive the world around you?

Are memories all born healthy?

Are some memories born disturbed?

So we can conclude that trauma has a tragic and effect on a well balanced memory.

Do memories get lonely?

Are memories born into the mind yet are an extension of reality.

How is a new memory created?

Is it through time, space, distance and foreseeing a new experience. Reminiscent.

Planning for the future and living in the present. Are memories independent of thought? Do memories have a mind of their own?

Do memories get tired?

Do memories get sick, physically emotionally? Do memories have a cardiovascular system and a neurological system?

Memories get sharper.

Some memories are dull.

Some memories are forgotten.

Some memories remain a concept in the mind and never make it to reality.

Are memories the cause of Alzheimer's?

Are memories the distortion of into profanity?

What is the definition of a memory?

A individual who can recall his location at any given time place even distance space and in the company other persons.

Memory is a physical manifestation..

A Poem By:

Nkosinathi 2Pistolz Ncala

The Formless Thought:
A thought free of judgement.
A thought yet to be born from understanding.
Wisdom flows from thy ways.
A thought yet to be conditioned by circumstances.
A thought yet to think.
A thought that only blinks when the eye needs to rest.
A thought is bound to the nature of the spirit.
Ultimately weather the light will outshine the darkness is a currency of morality versus the fallacy of the indomnibles.
Who inspects thought while it is in the mind?
Consciousness.
What drives a thought mad?
A cheating spouse or groom?
Debt.
Depression.
Hopelessness when faith is held captive by fear.
When the primary dream has died an unnatural death.
The power of the tongue.
One can speak upright just and fair.
Concealing what the heart thinketh.
Words are sweet betrayal is bitter.
Poison will shut down the nervous system it's a matter of time a matter of seconds between life and death.
Only in reality can a thought manifest.
While a thought lives in the mind it is a concept yet to be actualized.
Barriers of Thought:
Primarily fear suffocates thought?
One's perspective in retrospect is held at random by the thoughts we keep.

The well being of one's psychological state is in accord with the motives in their heart which are ultimately the transgressions in hindsight being your actions.

With sin.

The anamosity.

The beef runs deep in our veins.

It's time we settle the score.

Generation after generation after generation.

Will there ever be peace?

Is thought cursed?

Who put the mind under a spell?

Who is the master of thought?

Ultimately where is thought headed?

What is destiny is rehearsed?

What if our fate is in the hands of the government?

What if?

What about God?

As a thought is forming.

What are the ingredients which determine what form of shape the thought will take?

The mind.

The immediate physical environment.

The external environment the pressures from society.

The psychological pressure.

What makes one thought superior to the next?

On which grounds does thought stand?

In the Battle for the domination of the mind who has the higher grought? Motive or thought.

The Formless Thought.

Nkosinathi 2Pistolz Ncala

The Forming of Thought

What matters the most to you?

Inevitably adversity will snatch the grasp of your palm from it how does that reality make you feel?

Can thought reason beyond the confines of consciousness?

What is consciousness?

Energy confined within a space a prism called the mind. Within the mind lies segments of which consciousness will be streamlined and divided into sectors of thoughts instincts desires.

From consciousness we have dreams polar effect nightmares. Delicts of thought Alzheimer's and issues and the stigma of mental health.

So have established consciousness is independent of the mind. Yet they co exist for the organism to function and survive in reality.

Consciousness is biological..

Stress is mechanical a product of survival habitually there is famine in the land and animal or mankind can not pay the bond he just lost his job.

Stress is natural.

Stress is a force of nature.

Stress is neural primary at a glance neither positive or negative.

Yet stress unexamined can collapse the entire nervous system without an army and a coup. Stress is the dangerous by any imaginable extreme.

Pay close attention to the events in your life that may stress you. Study your mistakes that is the indigenous way to grow and turn tragedy to lessons.

Pressure is a force exerted internally.

Pressure is a force exerted externally.

Pressure is a for at the core of the organism biologically and intellectually.

Your inability to cope with pressure.

Your coping skills of pressure determine weather you will survive.

The underline the truth if the matter weather you will surpass the maindaine and great like those that came before you your ancestors.

What are the barriers to the development of thought? What enhances the advances of the ideology of thought propergating intellectual stimuli.

Primary 9 Fields of thought:

Academia.

Sports.

Politics.

Religion.

Criminology

The Judetary.

The Prison System and

Health care system.

The education system

The Conceptualization of The Forming of The Perfect Thought:
Close your eyes.
You have just feasted your iris on the
becoming's of a marvel.
A phenomenon.
A visual spectacle.
The saga continues.
Take a look through the Webb Hobbs telescope over 4000 years of astrology and scientific research in conglomerate of dozens of not hundreds of quadrant high definition lenses.

Given the data by range South Africa Weather Services you will be given the exact time day and year the sun and the moon will eclipse and the duration of time this miracle will last.

Don't blink to the east we have a star which is under going crystallisation a sub is being born.

Planets orbit the milky way at speeds of over 100 000 Kms per second yet are never knocked off their axis the mygesty of creation simply shows off its splendour when coming toe to toe with adversity.

There comes a commits 5;1 millions neon seconds per kilometre. bomb bang into an unnamed planet. There goes the peace. Can you interface make peace either way you gotta live with the rapture.

The galaxies gaze at solar systems discovering new planets. Moons or it the sun remaining synonymous with mystery.

Who sits at the top of the food chain of creation?
God.
Existence.
Salvation.
Wisdom and understanding.
Recreation.
The might and wit to procreate.
These are the gift of the spirit.
In the realm of science and logic.

Time reigns supreme.

Gravity regulates mass and weight.

Land water and air form under the stratosphere where clouds form the the rains fall and life is nourished and replenished as we know it.

Each diety has its way of life.

Human beings have a belief system.

The purpose of life is to visualise actualized and manifest your primary dream while permits in your lifetime.

What is the meaning of life?

What exists beyond the known world.

Beyond right and wrong surely beyond redemption life thrives free of the confines of yesterday.

The Conceptualization of The Forming of The Perfect Thought:
A Poem By:
Nkosinathi 2Pistolz Ncala

The Crystallization of Thought:

The see thought thought.

The naked mind.

The transparent action.

What you see is what you get.

By no means is this kid tame.

He is raw.

Unrefined.

Yet considerate.

Given a task he will blow the mind of the invigilators. Team work is of the essence. Yet as a lone hunter he is a deadly assassin.

The anointing of the ideology.

The sacrificing of motive.

The begetting of fear.

The crucifix of the unknown.

The baptism of doubt.

The burial of sin in one's lifetime.

The rise of the tyrannical.

The commands will sanctify the heart.

Cleansing the conscious of all the desires which clog the vision mission and sight of all that lies in the heart.

The mind is an instrument respect it. Study it. Grasp it. Understand it's power and unlearn it's weaknesses.

Beneath The Simulation

Consciousness Energy and Thought.

The pig the rat the cat the dog the cow the pest this is the primary domesticated animals that humanity interacts with habitually daily.

When it comes to meat we eat lamb, mutton, beef and chicken.

These animals are breed in captivity.

Primarily their lifespan and existence I'm the simulation is to be slaughtered.

Livestock are breed for consumption they born and lives breed and are slayed in captivity.

The grazing grounds are the playground.

The fate of the baby lamb is in the hands of the farmer.

Yet let us remember God Jesus Christ fed the hungry fish and bread.

By no means is anyone judging the system we observing analysing and gaining insight into the protocol on the status quo of the day in the life of a pawn.

Breed feed the highest quality of grazing land and served on a platter be it at home or in a restaurant or resort.

Now the human being with all mankind's wisdom and understanding is not fallible neither is his brother or neighbour exempt from suffering.

Prejudice oppression suppression of liberty the exiling of freedom from her native land of birth.

How does the soul communicate with the spirit. Primary is it though the mother tongue. Perhaps images projected as memories when we face the decision he human child is born into comfort or discomfort. Wealth will buy you privilege.

Suffering will test your faith and trust WILL to survive.

Where does one get the skills to go into combact with adversity altering your destiny and fate?

The dog is man's best friend.

Yet is still confined within the perimeter of the home and taken for walks depending on the commitment of the master.

Believe it or not.

In the game of domesticated animals.

The cat is king and queen.

The cat is not confined to the walls of the household.

The cat can catch and hunt wild birds at any given moment an other pray within its scope and them come home for the dog to eat perhaps for the master to marvel.

A Poem By
Nkosinathi 2Pistolz Ncala

The Presence of The Soul
The essence of thought.
The spirit.
The identity of the self.
The ego.
Consciousness is universe.
Trees shall bear fruits.
Shrubs shall sprout.
Crops shall be harvested.
Seasons shall transgress.
The climate is unpredictable.
The chronology of climatology.
The adverse nature of soil erosion.

Mountains determine the flow of the wind and the streams and rivers. How often the clouds form along the altitude of sunlight and photosynthesis how hard little or non rain fall shall fall on the planet earth.

Let there be life.

An organism is born within a habitat the environment shapes and determines the behaviour and diet of the organism.

Aquarians:

Fish.

Whales.

Sharks.

Dolphins.

These species live, breed, hunt and breathe under water. The depth and altitude of their habitat has not been explored in its entirety.

The ocean is vast.

Coral life shrouds in abundance there is enough vegetation for all to feast and indulge.

Reptiles

Are cold blooded by nature.

Live on land.

With the exception of the crocodile which live a on land and water.

Reptiles are difficult to tame.

Yet mankind is fascinated by these creatures. In not cases they lay eggs and do not birth their young. Their seeding's of reptiles are born all knowing.

Reptiles.

Hunt their prey.

Eat them alive.

They scaled.

They slither in the grass and swallow their prey whole.

Mammals.

Warm blooded.

Live on land.

Mate, hunt, breed eat according the evolution of their ecosystem and natural habitat.

The sad reality both mammals and reptiles live, breed and die in captivity.

Homsapians

Mate, breathe air and harvest their food through farming and irrigation.

Explore the continent and beyond the boarders of sea space and land.

They are Inventors with modern and future technologies should will shape reality.

A Poem By

Nkosinathi 2Pistolz Ncala

Sensory Precautionary Glands.

The ingestion of existence.

Consciousness.

The organism is born lives and dies.

While you live you must survive.

The mind is reminded of its greatness everytime it's thinks. The mind is a mirror a reflection of the soul. The spirit breathes. While the being lives death larks in the shadows.

What do you fear? The force of life verses the force of death?

The human being prepares it's food.

Primarily the vegetarian and the meat lover. Ingestion of food, digesting food and the passing of solid waste outside the body.

We naturally eat for dietary purposes to sustain the organism and to stay alive.

Reproduction is generationally to reproduce. Yet mankind is a complex organism. We have developed language linguistics and communication we have industrialised the planet earth and its resources.

Yet have the libido which is an indicator of your sexual appetite how often you have sex your preferred way of in gauging in sex. How many sexual partners you have at any given time.

Most importantly are you heterosexual bisexual or homosexual?

They say be weary of the food you eat.

It can bring you health or disease.

The nature of the spirit weather one is of the light or a reflection is predominantly determined by the thoughts they keep.

Laziness or a fruitful nature.

Yet what is the cause of disease.

We know sexually transmitted diseases are primarily acquired through lucid sex.

Mental unwellness is triggered by trauma PTSD and manifest as depression.

The soul is trapped in a cycle of survival the slave master is money.

You work so hard for your money.

How do you spend your money?

Are you saving and investing enough money? Have you figured a way to curb and reduce expenses?

How do you multiply your sources of income? What are your avenues of multiplying your immediate income base?

Sight the gift of vision the forming of the image.

Hearing the content of understanding wisdom and the art of knowing.

Touching bridging the gap between mind and matter.

Thinking pondering and bringing front the metaphysical to the world of life the world of the living.

A Poem By

Nkosinath 2Pistolz Ncala

The Moon Is A Reflection of The Earth During The Day. The Sun Comes Alive When The Moon Is Asleep.

At night the moon is the ocean.

The telekinesis between moon earth and ocean water precipitation gave rise to the sun.

Let there be light.

Water is the source of life.

Water is a gas.

Water is a liquid.

Water can be also transform under the right temperature & pressure becomes a solid.

Water is primarily made of oxygen and hydrogen. These are noble gases range within room and body temperature.

The sun is the source of sunlight.

Yet the moon is the mother of water.

The existence of the sun and moon conceived planet earth by design or hook perhaps by the evolution of time.

The belly of consciousness is as vast as the ocean. In reality can the mind ever grasp the potential of thought? If it was not for the pressures of stress. Perception would lift the whiskers off poverty and tell the man to rise above adversity.

Circumstantially it's never too late to start again yet in the battle to succeed it is easier said then done.

Pick your enemies carefully where possible. The betrayal is always murky even if you suspect and see it coming you blinded by trust. A broken heart is the price you pay for loyalty.

Love at your own risk.

How do you mend a broken heart.

When you fall catch your breath and get up. Cross nobody on your way to the top.

Even a troop of ants will rise up against an elephant.

In retrospect consciousness is not what it may seem. The inner eye and the external vision. What the heart thinks and what the mind sees may not be aligned with the content of your consciousness.

The beauty of yesterday can not die even though it is free of breath. Tomorrow is buried alive. The now has just been born a mind with a state of mind yet alive and weather the probabilities of success outweigh failure is solely inte hands of fate the palm within your hand is destiny.

Let go of your past.

There is nothing to fear.

Revenge is a coward.

Make peace with your past.

Build a modern safe heaven for the angels living on earth.

Humanity needs a Prayer.

Will God answer it?

Well that depends on your needs.

Most importantly will your prayer reach God? Only time will tell.

A Poem By

Nkosinathi 2Pistolz Ncala

The Sun The Moon Water

Magma Optus

The Heavens Simmer Above The Sun.

The pupil of creation.

The iris of the unknown.

Life orbits the placenta of the universe.

Destiny remains a mystery time is in the hands of fate. Creation is the splendour of reproduction.

Choose your mate carefully.

Your heritage primarily rests in the faith of your partner's heart. The honour of a faithful heart is scorned upon your peers.

The disgrace of dishonour is the ultimate humiliation before a snared death.

The Sun.

Light.

The source of laver and magma.

Resonating with motion.

The moon.

When night falls the light amongst the shadows.

Whining.

Waves.

A frequency which communicates with the ocean.

Water.

The mother of life.

Hydrogen an oxygen.

A product of the interface between the Sun and moon.

Over the centuries life is conceived.

The natural habitat.

The sky.

The lens of the Gods.

Times captures the memories.

One moment at a time.

A cloud forms and disappears at an instance before you can swallow your breath.

The gift of life is conceived.

A baby is born.

9 months 2 days.

Weighing 2.3 kgs

It's a girl.

It's a boy.

It is twins.

What is the source of life?

How does energy form?

Consciousness projects thought

The reflection of the light

is a spectrum of darkness.

Freedom is an instrument of liberty.

The spirit is living.

The shadow is dead.

The heart is deceitful.

The mind thinketh.

The flesh is meek.

The dead are unable to speak, haunting.

Thought reflect consciousness.

Health and illness are the radar of immunity.

A Poem By

Nkosinathi 2Pistolz Ncala

The Soul Is The Flesh of The Spirit.

Thoughts Born In Captivity.

Can science and religion give a precise explanation factually historically, how was consciousness conceived?

Could destiny have been a reality before consciousness was born?

What is the catalyst that led to consciousness forming? What are the biological conditions needed for consciousness to come to life?

Psychologically

What separates consciousness from thought?

What is the destiny of a thought born in the realm of consciousness?

The thought is free of motive.

What is the fate of a thought born in the mind? The thought is a slave to thinking.

These are thoughts that are born in captivity.

Born a dream.

Live in the mind.

Die in reality.

Live forever as the constitution of democracy the liberty of freedom.

If heaven is the supreme thought.

God is the manifestation of consciousness.

If so what is the anointing and the presence of fate on the destination of the soul?

The soul can not die. No.

The spirit can not be born yet it lives.

So death is an illusion.

Birth is a manifestation.

Reproduction is the primary instinct bring us closer to being the procreators.

Have you ever seen the reflection of God? Look in the mirror you are a reflection of the son of man.

The spirit manifests the burdens of the flesh. The temptations of desire.

The will of discipline. The contempt of sin. The curiosity embedded in the suspense of danger.

Can the life be separated from the simulation? Life and consciousness are they separated at birth and united upon the death of the flesh and the liberation of the soul.

The spirit, the soul, life the platform of existence. Consciousness the instrument bridging the gap between mind dreams thought anxieties doubts aspirations and the reality y of heaven and hell.

You are either living or dying.

Passive thriving or resisting.

A reflection of God.

Yet there is no shadow that is reflecting.

The soul has authority over what lies in the mind. The soul lives in the heart. As blood flows through my veins. The souls breathes through my thoughts exhaling through my deeds.

Long after you gone your reputation lives on, beyond the grave. Can forgiveness look beyond the deed? Remorse and repentance are key in the fellowship of forgiveness. Salvation is not promised.

How does one attain salvation and keep it till their dying days.

So life breeds beyond the blood after all.

If love is a feeling and falling in love means I have to trust and open up my heart I'm clutching on to my heart where there is trust there is betrayal. Watch out for the dagger there comes the upper cut.

A Poem By

Nkosinathi 2Pistolz Ncala

Is Consciousness Universal?

Is thought a product of consciousness?

The mind thought and environment.

The Becoming of Thought.

(Capture The Image Before It Becomes A Thought).

Consciousness declassified.

What is the supreme Thought?

Does anything regime absolutely above God manifest? Can any form of life independent of God Manifest?

Does existence fall within the spectrum of the universe soley.

Is creation independent of God?

Is God independent of creation?

In your own understanding how would you define good? In your own knowledge what is your perception of creation?

Can you seperate God from creation? Can creation be seperated from God?

Without consciousness can there be life?

Capture the image before it becomes a thought.

For once the image has formed the sub conscious mind is forming in the background. The mind is under siege the positive thought and the negative thought are forming simultaneously.

The more frequent thought will dominate the other. Meaning. If your mind is occupied with darkness all day negative thought will rule the analogy of your thought.

If your thoughts are positive all day.

Your psychology of thought will lean on positivity.

It is only a matter of instinct and time that motives will take over the mind.

What is more powerful instinct thought. or motive?

As only these principles know the content of your brain in its entirety.

Well let us examine the content of the human mind survival. The battle to stay alive. The infestation of thought verses the tranquility and equilibrium of balance efficiency and peace.

What seperated one thought from the next? Are thoughts bio laterally uniform?

Do thoughts on a cellular level have the same genometric structure?

At what stage do thoughts form their own ideologies and go their seperate ways? Do thoughts relate on a social level are thoughts social enzymes?.

Do some thoughts form bonds that will last a lifetime?

Are some thoughts born atheists?

Are some thoughts drawn to faith?

Are some thoughts lonely?

Does each and every thought that existed in the mind have a biological parent?

Some thoughts are innovative.

Some thoughts are depressed.

Some thoughts are suicidal before they reach adolescents mental wellness.

Is thought universal.

Weather you reptile mammel acquarian mountain river ocean planet galaxy star milky way sun or moon.

The basic characteristics of existence.

Genetics.

Formation of species or tribe.

Accumulation of data information evolution and the species grows survives and survives global warming and climate change.

There are primarily 2 types of thought a positive thought and and negative thought. As an individual all aspects of projection of consciousness. You are either moving forward stagnent or non progressive moving backwards.

The combinations of thought are limitless.

How many thoughts do you have in a minute? How many thoughts do you have in a hour, a day, a week, a month.

Can you remember how many thoughts you had last year?

How many thoughts have you had since you have were born?

What is it important to be cognizant of the nature of thoughts one harness and harvests?

One day the thought will make the transition from the mind to reality.

Some dreams never form.

Some dreams remain conceptual.

Some dreams suffocate under pressure and do not develop coping skills to survive let alone manifest in reality.

A Poem By
Nkosinathi 2Pistolz Ncala

Climatology & The Well Being of Our Planet:
Nature exists independent of man.
Yet the incarnation of AI
Artificial Intelligence is solely breed by mankind and his accumulated understanding.
What is the source of energy for climatology?
The sun, the moon, the ocean the solar system.
What is the source of life?
Does breath have a life-force?
What is analogy of breath?
The suspense in breathing.
The interception in breathing.
The relief in exhaling.
Where there is breath there is life.
Let there be growth.
The shadow forms because of the presence of matter, mass casts an image reflecting physical appearance.
The soul is the identity of the spirit.
Yet what gave breath to the reproduction of creation and life.
God.
The Wondering Eye.
The rains.
The clouds bring the rains.
The drought.
The deserts brew the days
where the rains are few and far apart.
The tsunami.
Abnormal sea tides and high sea level and giant waves.
The storms.
A serge of the rains.
The solar system.
Planets are aligned geometrically.

Fixed to the axis which they rotate around a gravitational form for their entire existence.

The order of the universe is infinite.

Who dares to question what time the sun should rise and set? This season will winter be late will summer be on time. No one knows for sure.

Yet the bio degradable chemicals we release into the atmosphere are scientifically proven to speed up the process of climate change.

The Concept of The Afterlife

The Carbon Footprint of The Shadow:

The Kingdom of Thought:

Measure your ways a metre echo's a thousand miles. Wage your words the tongue will set the heart on fire.

Without your consent you have waged a war against your own mind.

Forget the concept of peace you about to witness the great depression.

The hierarchy of greatness.

Glory to the mighty.

May peace have mercy on the dearly departed. Your reputation lives on long after you are belated.

Is a thought born a slave.

Another thought is born a master.

The mind is the plantation.

Without hesitation the speculation of choice will bewilder consciousness into retracting into a conceptual form.

The world thought is born into.

We are not referring to the geographical landscape. Thought manifests in the mind forming images. How does a image form?

How many thoughts does it take to form a single image? What came first the image or the thought? Perhaps that is irrelevant. The image is the embryo the thought is the birth of the organism.

The seed and fruits of the tree carry the DNA embedded in the roots.

The imagination is ultimately concealed in the memory embedded in remembrance. Your ability to recall the date place time environment and people is in the essence the clarity of the memory.

A Poem by

Nkosinathi 2Pistolz Ncala

How Did Words Come Alive?

Where do words originate from?

In the bigger picture what is the role of words in the advancement of communication, language and intelligence?

Were words singular at point of their existence? What is the catalyst for the expansion of words into vocabulary.

Words of 2024 are so advanced we have over 200 languages nations and +-

2 000 tongues.

L

Well it is written.

In the beginning was the word and the word was God and the word was with God. And the God was God.

Genesis Chapter 1.

Essentially what are words?

They are the bridge between consciousness and dreams.

Words the medium used to communicate between thoughts in transit.

The hierarchy of thought.

The struggle to survive.

What determines the characteristics of thought? Which thoughts will come alive.

Which thoughts have potential to thrive in reality? Which Thoughts will remain meek?

Which thoughts will come alive and shape the community society beyond our immediate surroundings.

Can you spot a thought?

What is the sequence words gather in to form a sentence linguistically?

What is the importance of thought?

What is the significance of words.

What is the catalyst that shifted and precipitated the evolution of the word to words thus communication intelligence linguistics. We have over 200 nations over 2 000 tongues of ethic tongues around the continent and world.

In the past 100 years what advances have been made in the field of language

words and linguistics. AI and academia sports politics are advancing.

Yes Amazon pays authors 51 million dollars months.

Yet is the art and science of words growing as a field which is the skeleton

for the establishment knowledge and understanding as we know it in 2024.

A Poem By
Nkosinathi 2Pistolz Ncala

When The Borders of The Mind Collapse

What is left of consciousness?

Have you ever seen a naked thought?

Were your senses aroused.

Did you figuratively climax?

Within the structure of the cell there is absolute order. No coincidences, no mistakes no mishaps there is complete order.

Destiny is in the hands of the sword.

Yet in the day of the final battle the victor is not necessarily on ground advantage yet whom the weather is conducive too and whole the terrain favours.

The most skilled warrior is not necessarily the most gifted. One who a strategist an illusionist seemingly enabled to manipulate time.

The Circular Pyramid

Drifted out sight of the radar of consciousness while the mind was fast asleep. Only for the Pharaoh and the chief magicians and elders to wake up after the great annual feast.

Only to realise the goddesses of Babylonia and Ethiopia pulled a hoax on them again and again century after century after century. From the old Kingdom the middle kingdom the new kingdom there is nothing new under the sun.

This befalls the great kingdom of Egypt again and again and again. The power of the cake. For Egypt the circular pyramid is equivalent to the ark of God with the coveninent with mankind.

Beneath the moon.

There is no vascular life above the sun.

Where ever clouds form there are the rains lightning storms droughts and a geographical landscape the light reflecting moisture precipitation and life.

Clouds are the pupil the iris of creation.

The simulation takes beneath the sun.

Where ever there is gravity there is life.

As far as science has experimented gravity is a force subject to the manifesting and harvesting of life on mother earth.

What lies above the sun no one knows for sure. All forms of life that cast a shadow exist on a molecular level?

Life branches into different segments of being on a cellular level.

What separated one field of energy from another? Mitosis.

Even the seed branches into different forms of lush vegetation shrubs and fruits.

The ovaries are fertilized by the sperm the reproductive organs and juices of mammals reptiles and humans carry the DNA inherently the genetics and detailed fate of souls yet to be born.

Wisdom, knowledge, understanding is circular with no beginning recorded in mankind's written existence and no ending in sight there is no summit when it comes to research and the gathering of data an information.

Fear predominantly is an eminent phobia. Laughter releases the tension and eases the stress. When the fatigue is building up rest. Take a break from the rat race ever so often it will do your spirit much jubilation.

The essence of life is progress on all fronts of existence or you will have a bottomless void which can only be filled by success and victory of dreams coming to life in reality leaving you mind a fertile breeding ground for more dreams to be conceived.

A Poem By
Nkosinathi 2Pistolz Ncala

Brazen Lies Scattered Dreams

Can You Conceal The Truth?

For how long with the chosen nation and tribe of God suffer?

Where the holy books written to set us free? Where the holy books written to enslave us?

What constitutes a lie?

What depicts the truth?

Can you tell the difference between a lie and the truth?

The truth is bare.

The truth is naked.

The truth has nothing to hide.

Lies are hard to detect.

Lies hide behind motives.

Lies are the enemy they conceal the truth. Lies are buried in the heart.

Lies give rise to paranoia.

Doubt rages like the truth know deceit is in the mists of thoughts how can you escape reality, you have to face your destiny or you will awake stress and under subdued pressure depression is awakened.

When in the depths of your heart you know you have wrong another human being you feel guilty. Unresolved guilt manifests into shame. Where there has been a transgression sin remorse repentance forgiveness are the salvation of the day.

So lies and truth manifest from thought.

What came first truth or lies?

What is factual truth or lies?

Which is a constructive or potentially distractive force truth or lies?

In dialouge you are either narrating a story.

You are either telling the truth or lying.

The truth is the only that exists.

Lies are shadows of existence which do not have a direct source of light as they shine from a point of darkness of cause they will reflect shades of darkness.

When You See Through Thought You No longer Blinded By The Mirrors of Reality:

Perception I see there I form images in the mind. Memories form a cellarage of remembrance to forget is a fallacy now can you see beyond the boundaries of thought?

My ears translate sounds from the environment. The dogs are barking are they playing? Are the dogs Hollowing at the moon? is it danger is it night time are we in the mists of bandits and strangers?

My nostrils are refined to the taste of my favourite cosine. The sent of my girl friend arouses my senses putting me in the mood for four play which will lead to intimacy.

My tongue to taste, to indulge to devour let's explore the wonders of 5 star dishes.

The sensation of touching to feel to exalt to be in the physical presence of greatness

.

Let us look closely at the platform called the mind. Open up consciousness what do you find? Thought. Within thought lies a world of parallels. Extracts of paradigms longitudinal lines gravitating towards the centre of your deeps desires.

The centre of fear is rooted in the unknown. Doubt plays on paranoia. The inability to make up your mind leads to speculation and hesitation. A smile quickly turns into a frown in the face of adversity.

Consciousness is the throne on which thought sits upon. Energy Rae energy creation in its purest forms. Incarnations into the cell of a living thought. Life is of the essence.

Some thoughts are yet to be born.

Some dreams are yet to form.

There can be no motives where there is no intention. Thought needs to have a destination and purpose for motive to manifest.

Pain is excruciating.

Pain is uncomfortable.

Nobody wants to be in pain.

Pain is a symptom that that is a void or unwanted enzyme harmful cell or the tissue or flesh of the skin has been temporarily or permanently penetrated God forbid a limb has lost through a accident or terminal illness.

Psychological pain.

Physical pain.

Emotional turmoil.

Financial embezzlement.

Not knowing who to trust.

Doubling your instincts.

Not having a personal relationship with ship with God will leave you vulnerable to spiritual attacks. You may draught your personal growth. Block your blessings from your ancestors and angels.

A Poem By

Nkosinathi 2Pistolz Ncala

When You See Through Thought You No longer be Blinded By The Mirrors of Reality

A Poem By

Nkosinathi 2Pistolz Ncala

The Day Cometh When Shadows Will Be Independent of The Flesh:

AI Artificial Intelligence the rise of the bots is unfolding before our naked eyes in 2024. Machine learning and automation.

Si Spiritual Intelligence is hibernating in the back ground. Studying every step the human being makes. Measuring every breath. Calculating every thought. Analysing every error in judgement.

The shadow is building its own mind.

A fortress free of thought.

No mind.

No heart heartless motive has no place to call home.

The Is a state of a dream.

The combinations are endless.

Destiny is limitless.

Fate is brisk it can cut life short now.

Yet the miracle of consciousness is alive and can not meet a demise of the flesh for it is a force of energy driven by the breath of creation itself.

How will shadows live in the future?

How I'll they breed?

What will they eat?

Will they astro project?

Will shadows learn how to time travel?

Will they invent a better simulation more just then reality?

Is a day coming when shadows will turn against mankind?

Mankind pays no attention to the shadow while he lives. He disregards it's presence. Neither acknowledging it in prayer or daily rituals.

There are very few stories books or conversations on a daily basis on shadow. The shadow is an outcast. It is not recognised as a living organ.

The shadow breathes the air that I breath. The shadow hurts when I am in pain. When jubilation is in my soul the shadow echo's besides my laughter.

Remember the day I was created when my mum and dad's shadows were do close they were not just making love. Their universes aligned and my shadow would form in the womb a replica of my dad's mother and my mum's father's.

Here is am yet to replicate the miracle.

Pay attention to the mood of your shadow. When your shadow is asleep be awake. Ying when you awake your shadow is awake. The sun and moon water and earth.

Fear not the knowledge of the occult.

Strive for independence.

Demystify the unknown.

Find truth and relevance in a hopeless situation that is the only way to unseat adversity.

Remember these words in your darkest night.

There will be no white flag raised on this ship.

A Poem By
Nkosinathi 2Pistolz Ncala

The Cerebellum of Thought

The nuclei centred around the process called thinking. The inner circle of thought can only be penetrated by thought. Thoughts enter the brain with no state of mind.

Thought is born with no perception.

The agility of thought determines how efficiently thought will grow. Yet weather your thoughts will be inclined to the darkness or light rests with your subconscious.

The heart is a reflection of paranoia a synthesis of your fears doubts and anxieties. Listen to your thoughts before they become motives.

There are a limitless combination of thought. The possibilies of thought are limitless. Mind you there are primarily 2 thoughts a positive thought and a negative thought.

The laws of nature one thought will dominate the other. The thought that dominates the weaker thought ultimately suffocates it disregards it as passive waste or enslaves it is a decoded enslaved memory using it as intellectual fuel on the Transmission from mind to reality.

Once thought has taken over the mind.

The spirit and the soul have to move forward physically financially and psychologically. The thought that masters all disciplines of life health

The comfort of wealth, career, relationships, religion, politics, sports and academia.

This thought will ultimately conquer its enemies and enlarge it's territory.

The manifestation of thought is the projection of images into existence.

How do you know that you living?

Keep breathing.

When your back is against the wall.

This offence strategy is easier said then. Comprehended. When under inconceivable pressure how does one soak up the pressure?

Stand on your toes and look adversity in the iris. In order for this technique to work you need to have tamed your aggression.

A skilled Chaldean is aware the weaker the opponent conserve your energy and technique for another day another battle.

To win the battle without raising the sword is more noble then then a battle won an the king was slay.

A Poem By
    Nkosinathi 2Pistolz Ncala

When You See Through Thought You No longer Blinded By The Mirrors of Reality:

Perception I see there I form images in the mind. Memories form a cellarage of remembrance to forget is a fallacy now can you see beyond the boundaries of thought?

My ears translate sounds from the environment. The dogs are barking are they playing? Are the dogs hollowing at the moon? Is it danger is it night time are we in the mists of bandits and strangers?

My nostrils are refined to the taste of my favourite cosine. The sent of my girl friend arouses my senses putting me in the mood for four play which will lead to intimacy.

My tongue to taste, to indulge to devour let's explore the wonders of 5 star dishes.

The sensation of touching to feel to exalt to be in the physical presence of greatness

.

Let us look closely at the platform called the mind. Open up consciousness what do you find? Thought. Within thought lies a world of parallels. Extracts of paradigms longitudinal lines gravitating towards the centre of your deeps desires.

The centre of fear is rooted in the unknown. Doubt plays on paranoia. The inability to make up your mind leads to speculation and hesitation. A smile quickly turns into a frown in the face of adversity.

Consciousness is the throne on which thought sits upon. Energy Rae energy creation in its purest forms. Incarnations into the cell of a living thought. Life is of the essence.

Some thoughts are yet to be born.

Some dreams are yet to form.

There can be no motives where there is no intention. Thought needs to have a destination and purpose for motive to manifest.

Pain is excruciating.

Pain is uncomfortable.

Nobody wants to be in pain.

Pain is a symptom that that is a void or unwanted enzyme harmful cell or the tissue or flesh of the skin has been temporarily or permanently penetrated God forbid a limb has lost through a accident or terminal illness.

Psychological pain.

Physical pain.

Emotional turmoil.

Financial embezzlement.

Not knowing who to trust.

Doubling your instincts.

Not having a personal relationship with ship with God will leave you vulnerable to spiritual attacks. You may draught your personal growth. Block your blessings from your ancestors and angels.

A Poem By

Nkosinathi 2Pistolz Ncala

When You See Through Thought You No longer be Blinded By The Mirrors of Reality

A Poem By

Nkosinathi 2Pistolz Ncala

Calculate The Perimeter of Infinity:

Within the universe lies the consciousness of thought. Galaxies are living ancestors one day piece by piece they will be metros headed for the apocalypse of all planets with life.

Collecting all living entities with a soul one by one. Judgement has no remorse and reservations in sins which were committed bluntly or with lack of insight.

Ignorance will cost you dearly.

Before you burn the bridge called forgiveness think twice.

The boarders of eternity are measured by destiny. Fate is the instrument of time.

Numbers are divine. The alphabet is magical. How else would mankind communicate if it was not for these instruments.

What is the distance between 2 thoughts? What tool is used to measure the distance between 2 stars? How many years does it take for a star to form and ultimately be born.

On average how long does a star live? When does a start dying. Isn't that beautiful make a wish there comes a falling star shooting across the African sky.

The reflection of the sun is light.

Within light shadows lark darks looms like a daunting thought waiting to break free from the misery of depression.

The mind is dangerous learn it's patterns habits and weaknesses. Thoughts can construct and destruct the mind with a series and sequence of well calibrated constructs of ideologies which form perceptions which regulate the thinking process.

A thought is a reflection of its conditioning. A thought is not independent of scrutiny from judgement. A thought is an organism. It is born it lives and it's dies.

The thought can leave the mind upon a dream coming true and live longer then the mind and human being. The thoughts breathes information is fed data and is persuaded by emotions and the thought catches feelings.

When the thought can not make up its own mind thought doubts hesitates and slurs with no words let alone thoughts to express how it feels.

Father God Watch Over My Deliverance

Lord in times of trials and tribulations may my faith seek refuge in you.

May my hope summon the presence of the holy spirit from the heavens.

In the mists of the war in my mind the battle for perimeters and space in my heart may the dove of peace surface above my shadow a continent shadow.

Strengthen my weakness.

Grant me solitude in the mists of my humiliation and despair. Show me mercy my sin was in the mists of remorse. Surely forgiveness shall follow me all the days of my life.

May my pride be consumed by my desire may my bride walk along the road to my salvation. May our union be so sacred that death will make us mourn till we unite eternally as angels only to be born again in the flesh of the holy spirit.

Silence my anxieties. Lay void my doubts exterminate my fears. Depression will not be planted in the plantation called my mind.

We as the flesh spirit and metaphysical will uproot all segments and traces of darkness from within the boundaries and outside the boarders of our mind.

Consciousness has been contaminated by ty troubles of the world. Our problems outweigh our dreams in the battle field in this game of life everything is nothing like why it seems.

The only way to get closer to evil in the physical is to go blind with the eyes of the flesh. Open up the mind of the heart. And travel to the gates of heaven. While the being pumps blood in the living veins.

Obstacles and challenges mascarade as your friends how close you? How deeply do you care for them do they really love you unconditionally?

How well do you know your God?

Besides prayer what is your medium of communication with God?

How often do you talk to him does he respond when you call his name how often?

On the premises of becoming.

Father God Watch Over Deliverance.

Waiver my passions.

Summon my weakness and grant me my solitude. Father I beg of you guide me. May I never stray from your path.

May your light shine through the consciousness of my existence all the days of my life.

My living wishes.

One day when my flesh has faked my heart beat and life no longer lives in my blood may I serve in the house of the Lord.

As I Walk Towards My Salvation:

Father can hear me?

God do you feel me?

Mama shed no tears you represented the family and angels while you walked on earth. And Ima represent 144 000.

Angel number145.

Government name Nkosinathi 2Pistolz Ncala.

We got a new breed of angels Living amongst us 2047

Seraphim's are being breed in state captivity in the name of academia science and making advances in research methodology.

The road to redemption was never meant to be easy. For who ever has seen the truth will lose their desire the flesh is a mirage look carefully at what lives in your mind you will find your heart. Define motives. What would you define as the probabilities seeking first the kingdom of God?

Where can one purchase righteousness?

Am I in good standing with the Lord?

Is it even possible for a living entity to be in the physical presence of the almighty God?

Father i seek your favour above the wealth of the experience gained in the reality of understanding the wealth of my experiences as a mere mortal.

As I Walk Towards My Salvation:

What time is it father?

It's time for you to say your prayers.

Our Father Which Art In Heaven Hallowed Be Your Name...

Nkosi...

I said it's time for you to say your prayers.

Acoustic Angel.

She is an acoustic Angel.

Her halos they glow in the dark and illuminate hope in the light.

She's a spirit that is nolonger breathing.

She is nolonger waiting to exhale.

She is nolonger attached to the material world. Enlightenment mind she sees the future. She lives in the world of the present her memories they live in the world of the past past past.

She's deep but she ain't nothing like whoredom.

She grew up in the wilderness of sub Saharan Africa she's an African and in her afterlife she was born black again.

She speaks to me in tongues and wraps a web across my concentration span she's one with the creator of mankind.

She is what a princess is to a prince.

A king and his kingdom.

A mother to her daughter.

A father to her son.

A wife and her husband.

She is style.

She is grace.

She is fame.

She is acoustic angel.

Father.

God.

Dad.

Lord Jesus Christ

Mum

Mum

Son.

I birthed you, you have done me proud thus far, God forbid you keep your eyes on the Kingdom of Heaven.

Stray not from you salvation

I have others duties to attend to in the Heavens. Remember Even in The Darkest Night May The light of Your PLANS & Existence Shine Through The Darkness.

Now representative the angel regime

144 000

Angel number 145

Son.

Represent my Nigger.

Joyce Thembani Ncala Angel

Number 2325.

Mum

Lastly.

Ha Ah.

Haibo.

No Son.

Don't ask me anything about Tupac Michael Jackson Aretha Franklin they here worshipping the Lord God Jesus Christ.

Remember

You can join them one of these good days.

Represent.

A Poem By Nkosinathi 2Pistolz Ncala

Dreams

What is the nature of dreams?

What is the content of a dream?

What is the source substance of dreams?

What are dreams made of?

What does it take for a dream to come to life?

How long does it take for a dream to form? What is the lifespan of a dream?

What is the source of the dream?

At what age does the human being have their first dream?

Should you have your first dream in the womb does that make you left handed will you have favour with destiny?

Should you have your first dream as adolescent will you be a genius will you attain the purpose of your dream as your dream was conceived after puberty.

Should you have your primary dream as an adult is it too late to manifest or all that experience in life will come in handy?

What is the purpose of dreams?

Are dreams an extension of consciousness? Are dreams the umbilical cord of thought? Are dreams bilateral to destiny? Are dreams independent of fate judged by adversity.

The conspiracy of survival can not be undermined your circumstances can never be taken lightly ultimately they shape your reality.

Forms of Dreams

The past.

The present.

The future.

Primary these are the 3 states of dreams.

The universe is parallel adjacent to the longitudinal contour equator the dome of the mind. No thought leaves the mind destined for reality without consent of the prime consciousness.

Under no circumstances can dreams phonicate with thought that is the transgression where there will be no forgiveness death by dishonour.

Number your thoughts.

The more you know about the content in your mind. The less prone you are to spiritual attacks. Manipulation exploits your vulnerability and controls your impulses controlling you with the instrument of fear.

Financial defence and psychological impairment are the traits the scenario victim and the abuser.

The only way to kill a dream is to not believe it. Thus you deny the right to exist. The dream will remain in the concept of thought and die in the mind ultimately the memory of a dying or dead dream will clinically depress you.

A Poem By Nkosinathi 2Pistolz Ncala

Father God Watch Over My Deliverance

Lord in times of trials and tribulations may my faith seek refuge in you.

May my hope summon the presence of the holy spirit from the heavens.

In the mists of the war in my mind the battle for perimeters and space in my heart may the dove of peace surface above my shadow a continent shadow.

Strengthen my weakness.

Grant me solitude in the mists of my humiliation and dispare. Show me mercy my sin was in the mists of remorse. Surely forgiveness shall follow me all the days of my life.

May my pride be consumed by my desire may my bride walk along the road to my salvation. May our union be so sacred that death will make us mourn till we unite eternally as angels only to be born again in the flesh of the holy spirit.

Silence my anxieties. Lay void my doubts exterminate my fears. Depression will not be planted in the plantation called my mind.

We as the flesh spirit and metaphysical will uproot all segments and traces of darkness from within the boundaries and outside the boarders of our mind.

Consciousness has been contaminated by ty troubles of the world. Our problems outweigh our dreams in the battle field in this game of life everything is nothing like why it seems.

The only way to get closer to evil in the physical is to go blind with the eyes of the flesh. Open up the mind of the heart. And travel to the gates of heaven. While the being pumps blood in the living veins.

Obstacles and challenges mascarade as your friends how close you? How deeply do you care for them do they really love you unconditionally?

How well do you know your God?

Besides prayer what is your medium of communication with God?

How often do you talk to him does he respond when you call his name how often?

On the premises of becoming.

Father God Watch Over Deliverance.

Waiver my passions.

Summon my weakness and grant me my solitude. Father I beg of you guide me. May I never stray from your path.

May your light shine through the consciousness of my existence all the days of my life.

My living wishes.

One day when my flesh has fauked my heart beat and life no longer lives in my blood may I serve in the house of the Lord.

As I Walk Towards My Salvation:

Father can hear me?

God do you feel me?

Mama shed no tears you represented the family and angels while you walked on earth. And Ima represent 144 000.

Angel number145.

Government name Nkosinathi 2Pistolz Ncala.

We got a new breed of angels Living amongst us 2047

Seraphim's are being breed in state captivity in the name of academia science and making advances in research methodology.

The road to redemption was never meant to be easy. For who ever has seen the truth will lose their desire the flesh is a mirage look carefully at what lives in your mind you will find your heart. Define motives. What would you define as the probabilities seeking first the kingdom of God?

Where can one purchase righteousness?

Am I in good standing with the Lord?

Is it even possible for a living entity to be in the physical presence of the almighty God?

Father i seek your favour above the wealth of the experience gained in the reality of understanding the wealth of my experiences as a mere mortal.

As I Walk Towards My Salvation:

What time is it father?

It's time for you to say your prayers.

Our Father Which Art In Heaven Hallowed Be Your Name...

Nkosi...

I said it's time for you to say your prayers.

Acoustic Angel.

She is an acoustic Angel.

Her halos they glow in the dark and illuminate hope in the light.

She's a spirit that is nolonger breathing.

She is nolonger waiting to exhale.

She is nolonger attached to the material world. Enlightenment mind she sees the future. She lives in the world of the present her memories they live in the world of the past past past.

She's deep but she ain't nothing like whoredom.

She grew up in the wilderness of sub Saharan Africa she's an African and in her afterlife she was born black again.

She speaks to me in tongues and wraps a web across my concentration span she's one with the creator of mankind.

She is what a princess is to a prince.

A king and his kingdom.

A mother to her daughter.

A father to her son.

A wife and her husband.

She is style.

She is grace.

She is fame.

She is acoustic angel.

Father.

God.

Dad.

Lord Jesus Christ

Mum

Mum

Son.

I birthed you, you have done me proud thus far, God forbid you keep your eyes on the Kingdom of Heaven.

Stray not from you salvation

I have others duties to attend to in the Heavens. Remember Even in The Darkest Night May The light of Your PLANS & Existence Shine Through The Darkness.

Now representative the angel regime

144 000

Angel number 145

Son.

Represent my Nigger.

Joyce Thembani Ncala Angel

Number 2325.

Mum

Lastly.

Ha Ah.

Haibo.

No Son.

Don't ask me anything about Tupac Michael Jackson Aretha Franklin they here worshipping the Lord God Jesus Christ.

Remember

You can join them one of these good days.

Represent.

N.i.g g.e.r

A Poem By Nkosinathi 2Pistolz Ncala

Dreams

What is the nature of dreams?

What is the content of a dream?

What is the source substance of dreams?

What are dreams made of?

What does it take for a dream to come to life?

How long does it take for a dream to form? What is the lifespan of a dream?

What is the source of the dream?

At what age does the human being have their first dream?

Should you have your first dream in the womb does that make you left handed will you have favour with destiny?

Should you have your first dream as adolescent will you be a genius will you attain the purpose of your dream as your dream was conceived after purberty.

Should you have your primary dream as an adult is it too late to manifest or all that experience in life will come in handy?

What is the purpose of dreams?

Are dreams an extention of consciousness? Are dreams the umbilical ot thought? Are dreams bilateral to destiny? Are dreams independent of fate judged by adversity.

The conspiracy of survival can not be undermined your circumstances can never be taken lightly ultimately they shape your reality.

Forms of Dreams

The past.

The present.

The future.

Primary these are the 3 states of dreams.

The universe is parallel adjacent to the longitudinal contour equator the dome of the mind. No thought leaves the mind destined for reality without concent of the prime consciousness.

Under no circumstances can dreams phonicte with thought that is the transgression where there will be no forgiveness death by dishonour.

Number your thoughts.

The more you know about the content in your mind. The less prone you are to spiritual attacks. Manipulation exploits your vulnerability and controls your impulses controlling you with the instrument of fear.

Financial depence and psychological imparement are the traits the scenario victim and the abuser.

The only way to kill a dream is to not believe it. Thus you deny the right to exist. The dream will remain in the concept of thought and die in the mind ultimately the memory of a dying or dead dream will clinically depress you.

A Poem By Nkosinathi 2Pistolz Ncala

Let Us Perhaps Take A New Look At The Strategy of Battle In The Game of Life.

On turning the other check.

Verily.

God Jesus Christ.

1 God teach 2 sister teach 3 brothers teach 4 sisters teach 5 brothers.

Turn the other cheek.

Verily Lord Jesus Christ.

How do your turn the other cheek?

Turn the other cheek in the long run it will save for your life.

Without any effort the plans of your nemesis are foils as the sun is rising.

What light come from any deed done in the darkness?

Forget an enemy let alone pray for them that they may find it in their hearts to forget you.

In turn whom ever I have wronged may they forgive me if all else fails me in the flesh may my redemption come from the spirit of the presence of the Lord Jesus Christ.

When you turn the other cheek.

You observe as a loved one reveals the nature of their heart. Remember you may come from the same womb yet you ultimately have a different destiny.

Turn the other cheek.

When you strike a loved one.

Forget an enemy pray for them one day in this lifetime may God make it right again.

You gain foresight on your depth your limits your circumference and you quickly learn how far can you go.

What is faith?

What is hope can you have one without the other? What is the significance of your life? What is the splendour of your adversity?

The relevance of persistence is determination. Waiver your contempt nolonger is exempt from the fortunes and misfortunes of the wheel of life. The proximity of forgiveness and resentment is a stone throw away way martyr and hero's are made off.

Remember a villain was once a hero.

Nobody want to fall.

Yet the gravity of humiliation keeps up moping and grounded on the floor.

Get up and face today there is no other moment to express yourself you can only create in the now you can only live today.

Learn to forgive your heart will be lighter.

You will turn be a light as feather you will attract your blessings and if you do not live longer. You will live a more appealing life.

Let Us Perhaps Take A New Look At The Strategy of Battle In The Game of Life.

A Poem By
Nkosinathi 2Pistolz Ncala

The One Who Strikes First In Combact Wages War To The God's?.

The proverbial saying pick your battles carefully. Some battles are meant to be observed and on in the mind. One can gain perspective and insight through observation.

The relevance of circumstances can never be taken for granted they shape the perimeter of our world. Our destiny is in the hands of fate. The speculation of perhaps what could have been what should have been evades the stimulate of the very process known as peace.

Peace can only breathe where there is not an ounce of hate. When a negative force and a positive force collide there is Tarrant. The fall of the king is the death of a god.

For who can comfort a mounting queen?

The fears of her people which will in turn strengthen her weaknesses. In turn the spirit of the king is awakened and watches over his nation.

The rains summon the droughts.

Nature has a silly sense of spite by nature.

Remember kings all kings the 17 kings of the 144 tribes share one blood line.

The birth of the first son is the problem.

The one who strikes first in combat wages on the God's?

What's beef?

What is the root of pain?

When did it turn into pain?

Why does it hurt so bad?

My heart bleeds.

Trust is the door that opens up the portal for betrayal. Who can smote a dead man? Who can feel your pain in the same sense as the one that birthed you?

Today we transgress what is the point of living in the past. Is the a Doctor? Does anyone know a psychiatrist who can wake up a dead memory? How do you give strength to a dying memory?

How is a memory conceived?

How long will a memory live?

When does a memory start dying?

The is life?

What is the relevance of living?

What are the prospects of dying?

Why do you hate me?

Yet I love you?

Or do I depend on you financially psychologically emotionally?

The victim versus the oppressor.

What do you see in me?

Is there a light you see in me.

Is there glory in my existence that outshines your colony.

Yet the question remains why would you want to suffocate my dreams?

What makes you God your ancestors?

The One Who Strikes First In Combact Wages War To The God's?.

Before you wage war on a loved one.

Can I live without the memory of your existence? We at war on earth. How could we find peace in heaven?

Leastly how do mum and dad feel about our rivalry? The blessings of grandma and grandpa are bestowed as living dreams.

Upon Victory We Have A New Kingdom:

Do not touch the structures of the kingdom for 12 moons. This will please the God's of the ancestors. Mercy is the currency of the heart. The spirit can not be sold that is an illusion the great hypnotist.

When the sword of the king has fallen.

Let the queen and kings men have their day in court and may their trail be swift and fair. Do not impose Marshall law on the masses. History this is their land of the natives by birth.

Preserve national artefacts.

Breed livestock.

Harvest crops.

Make sure the land is fertile.

Let there not be a Square mile of land that is Barron even in a draught.

When electing new governs may they have shadow ministers of the old regime.

Do not let the people of the land feel as though you have subdued their and imposes your God's on the divinity of their ancestors.

The less resistance from your subjects.

There will be peace in the land.

The mighty serpent was not slain it was kept in captivity.

When you are strong and need new ideas with caution before the mighty serpent is too old. It shall be allowed to breed in captivity this new energy neither of the light or darkness shall be conceived in the land.

Technology academia sports governance there shall be a new breed of thought a renaissance.

Never slay the king least he fall on his sword God forbid. Never fantasise about the queen. She will live in your mind and take over the regime of your heart. The throne of the cake can never be underestimated let alone taken for granted.

Never strike a stranger unless your life is in danger least you die.

The premises of remorse grants the bestowing of remorse on the fallacy of the bereaved. Remember just because someone is subdued under pressure it may put pressure on their decision making ability.

Yet a skilled marks man's know of you soak up the pressure you come out stronger then your adversary.

And still remain resolute. Lust not and you will kill the desires of the flesh one by one.

A Poem By
   Nkosinathi 2Pistolz Ncala

The Structure of The Molecule of Thought.

On a cellular level thoughts divide and multiply amongst themselves mitosis.

Thoughts are breed in the mind. Thoughts live in the mind. Dreams are conceived in reality yet the fate of thought is to die in the captivity of called buried dead.

While you are alive create.

Yet if if you content with consuming products and services watch as the possibilities of innovation pass you by, that is also fine.

The barriers of thought.

Thought is essentially naked.

Thought covers and cloths consciousness.

Consciousness is the identity of the soul.

The finger print of your spirit the bio matrix and the very image of the existence of God's presence in your essence and being.

Thought can never be undermined.

Thought will let us know exactly what the shadow is plotting. The man the shadow the shadow are the axis of the being which carries the body as long as you live.

Ponder on your mobile existence it will give you closure and insight on the belly of your appetite to over com adversity. The road to success may be the manifestation of a broken dream.

Not all dreams come alive the majority of dream are never born. Most dreams die in the mind. The dreams that make it to reality are faced with the adversity of survival. Thus the pressures of reality the simulation are not natural.

The natural instincts of survival thirst hunger and reproduction. Biologically these instincts are resources.

Thirst water and food.

Grow free in nature yet food needs to be processed and purchased at a supermarket with currency. There are primarily endless way to earn currency. Yet why are there so many improvised people on earth?

The system is triggered.

Will I ever be a million aire let alone a billion aire? The truth is not in effort alone yet the application and success of strategy being at the right place at the right time.

Reproduction mating falling in love starting a family.

Food, shelter and clothing.

What will my family eat where will we live how will we cloth our ourselves.

Does 90 percent of my child's education take place at school? At home are we passive let the children play we busy being busy.

The nature of thought.

Essentially thought is energy.

Thought needs to be moulded.

Thought is secluded and deliberation takes place to determine the frequency and intensity of a thought.

Will the thought make it to reality?

Will the thought thrive in reality?

Is the thought sound in judgement?

Not all thoughts can be trusted?

Some thoughts are vile?

Bile is the s creation of contamination of thoughts that were hazardous to the flow consciousness and would have corrupted the hard drive of your mind ultimately ultimately uttering your destiny.

The Structure of The Molecule of Thought.

Where is thought headed no one knows for sure.

A Poem By

Nkosinathi 2Pistolz Ncala

Energy A State of Consciousness

There are 3 states of energy

Consciousness is a compilation of memories formed over a life. The conscious exists before consciousness is conceived.

A soul has to have had a past life in order to exist subconsciously. Yet the mind is born with a blank state of mind upon conception. Free from prejudice or favour.

The 3 States of Energy:

Consciousness energy in a gas form.

Thought is energy in liquid form.

Action energy in a solid form.

Consciousness energy in a gas form.

The character of thought is forming.

The nature of the being consciousness will be mouldered and sculptured into by the process of thinking.

Thought is energy in a liquid form.

The birth of WILL.

Having to choose between right and wrong. This is the stage where dreams are forming. Destiny lapses with fate.

Thought is ready to leave the mind and live in reality welcome to your new home.

Action energy in the solid form.

Choices have consequences.

We have different believe systems.

We were raised in different households.

Some us are traumatised.

Some us are balances.

Some of us are fragile.

Some of us need a little more guidance and attention.

Energy is omnipotent.

Energy is everywhere at the same time at every geographical location simulcast defying the laws of the nature of physics.

The gravity of energy is the chemistry of existence.

The stance energy has upon entering reality is to survive. It is not that simple. The web of economics has detached the soul from the essence of the roots of being sole providers.

Mankind must depend on the state for food to breed and to earn a living. You are born in a hospital your child will ultimately be born in a hospital and given a birth certificate.

The home you stay in is subsidised by the bank. The education everything on the curriculum is beneficial to the government your mind remains a knight in a prism called the capitalistic agenda.

Th gets deeper.

Why is it so important that from the moment the baby is currently Conceived.

The spirit Is trapped in the human body.

Freedom liberty democracy are conceptually but and fair.

Yet in reality poverty rains sin is triumph crime escalating everytime the governor increases the repo rate.

Sin.

Remorse.

Repentance.

Forgiveness.

Only to go and sin again the fallacy of man.

Will there ever be peace?

Will there be a law passed in every country to ban poverty from breeding in society and can and it will be done, in out lifetime.

Energy A State of Consciousness
A Poem By
Nkosinathi 2Pistolz Ncala

Dreams II

What is the nature of dreams?

What is the content of a dream?

What is the source substance of dreams?

What are dreams made of?

What does it take for a dream to come to life?

How long does it take for a dream to form? What is the lifespan of a dream?

What is the source of the dream?

At what age does the human being have their first dream?

Should you have your first dream in the womb does that make you left handed will you have favour with destiny?

Should you have your first dream as adolescent will you be a genius will you attain the purpose of your dream as your dream was conceived after purberty.

Should you have your primary dream as an adult is it too late to manifest or all that experience in life will come in handy?

What is the purpose of dreams?

Are dreams an extension of consciousness? Are dreams the umbilical ot thought? Are dreams bilateral to destiny? Are dreams independent of fate judged by adversity.

The conspiracy of survival can not be undermined your circumstances can never be taken lightly ultimately they shape your reality.

Forms of Dreams

The past.

The present.

The future.

Primary these are the 3 states of dreams.

The universe is parallel adjacent to the longitudinal contour equator the dome of the mind. No thought leaves The mind destined for reality without consent of the prime consciousness.

Under no circumstances can dreams phonicate with thought that is the transgression where there will be no forgiveness death by dishonour.

Number your thoughts.

The more you know about the content in your mind. The less prone you are to spiritual attacks. Manipulation exploits your vulnerability and controls your impulses controlling you with the instrument of fear.

Financial dependence and psychological impairment are the traits the scenario victim and the abuser.

The only way to kill a dream is to not believe it. Thus you deny the right to exist. The dream will remain in the concept of thought and die in the mind ultimately the memory of a dying or dead dream will clinically depress you.

A Poem By Nkosinathi 2Pistolz Ncala

Five Questions Which Will Determine The Destiny of Gloria & Nkosinathiz Path On Earth Perhaps Ultering Fate.

1. Thoughts Lapse.

A. You purchasing a Range Rover for the comfort of the CHILDRENS Daily Commune.

2. The Interface of Dream

B. US purchasing a Home together in an estate 4 bedroom.

3. Let US Breed So WE Can Live ForEVer.

Would you like to conceive 2025

4. Gloria Picture

Would You Like To Get Married

No matter what life has thrown at us December 23 2025

Our Thoughts Lapse

Parallel universes now adjacent in the flesh. Your soul touches my spirit

I feel your presence. Your ego is free of instinct yet you remain raw you can never be tamed even in captivity.

How could I ever own you, you were never on sale. Could you ever put a price tag on the existence of God? What is the discipline in creation the divine order of chromosomes enzymes are stipulated in the procreation.

Neither is the ant mightier then the elephant. Who can regulate the order of thoughts that mankind keeps.

At birth we weep tears of joy.

In times of trial and despair we weep tears of sorrow. Who will comfort pain time the scab will heal any physical wound not serve enough for an amputation.

Yet when it comes to the nature of the spirit. Betrayal mourns till we seek and are granted revenge. Blood is on my hands. Sin on my mind judgement awaits the deed the transgress of the law has a stiff penalty.

Wake up you have been asleep for way too long. While you gone to work Love I'll remember to engrave in the children's psyche. Have your cookies dip them in some milk. Wash em down with a glass of water.

Remember child before bed after school and homework if I am around or mummy is at work. Have your cookies dip them in some milk. Wash em down with a glass water.

I know you miss mummy she is working 2 jobs so you can live in this spacious home and get a private education.

With every poem I write we get inches closer to getting you and your sister a title deed in your lifetime.

I love you daddy.

I love you too son.

Standwa Sam

Just because I am not in your presence does not mean you have evaded my conscious. You are constantly on rotation in my mind like a number 1 hit on the radio station.

She lives in my mind.

I dwell in her heart.

Just the mere thought of her penetrates my consciousness heavenly being made of the flesh I can not lust of thee it would be a sin.

To have you on my mind is a transgression against the angels I am a mere mortal. My love to be in your presence is of the essence. Our union is it relevance when the walls of the world come tumbling down you are of relevance.

I can't tell her no lie she is the truth.

She is so close to God she must be an angel.

A Poem By

Nkosinathi 2Pistolz Ncala

The Interface of Dreams

The instrument known as the mind.

The melody called consciousness.

A genre called thought embraced by a culture known as thinking.

Raw energy for we are the people of God.

Every living species that breeds under the sun.

Explain creation mitosis the splitting of atoms. The relevance of forever breeds in the now. The home of the molecule is the nuclei. The universe is the pupil of the axis of rotation of the very existence of creation.

Dreams dip in and out of reality.

Dreams change places with thoughts.

Dreams are masters of playing mind games. Who controls thought? Who controls the mind?

Does the mind control thought?

Or does thought control the mind?

Do dreams control thought?

The destiny of thought is destiny.

The fate dreams is the journey known as fate. The mind is the platform consciousness chooses to express itself.

Can you tell the difference between a thought a dream and the mind?

What are the lessons we can learn from the physical appearance of thought?

Have you studied analysed and understood the biology of the mind what is the importance of this aspect of the reality of your reality.

As the image is forming.

As the image is formed in the mind conceptually. The image will one day live in reality. The conflict in the world has one source the seed of thought planted in the mind by consciousness be careful motives breed when you are unaware when you are asleep.

What breathes life into the image?

How does the image come alive?

How is the image conceived in the mind?

How long does the image live in the mind before it is birthed in reality? Does the image have a higher self? Is the image bound to an afterlife?

How do images reproduce in the mind?

How do images reproduce in reality?

Images are impressionable images are visual by nature. Images can be brain washed. It does not take concentration or lapse there off to hypnotise an image.

What is the role of the image in relaying consciousness to the brain?

Atomic particles in the mists of the moment. Only in the moment can the power of creation manifest. The relevance Of truth is septic to lies. Religion never got in bed with politics. The nun never fell in love with governor.

The church needed funding thus the integrity of the church was compromised by man the fallacy of WILL can not undermined let alone taken for granted.

The Interface of Dreams
A Poem By
Nkosinathi 2Pistolz Ncala

Let Us Breed So WE Can Live Forever:

Through our children.

Perhaps.

We bestow our dreams that is a hell of a burden for any child born in comfort moderation or suffering.

Let Us Breed So we Can Live Forever.

We were created in the image of the God's. Have you ever looked at life through the lens of the eyes the God's.

What would you see?

Would you be glaring at the sun, would you go blind?

Would you attain supreme knowledge and understanding? Would you be touched by a holy ghost could life ever be the same again?

Death is illusive.

Death evades life until your final breath.

Who is the master of the soul?

Who summons death to collect the souls of the living beings?

Life is a mystery unravel it.

Which dreams will come to life leaving the platform called the mind ploughing the simulation called reality. Just as the child is born. The soul gains understanding with experience. The dream is identified with its destiny.

The intensity of the thought is driven by its motive. Complexity of the problem is divulged in the nature of the circumstances.

The relevance of the solution is the resolution of conflict before it escalates to beef and blood is drawn from the veins of the accused and the defendant.

Let Us Breed So WE Can Live Forever:

Anything born will live.

Anything living must die.

In order to be born you must die.

So the concept of birth is creation.

Life has evolved to a simulation known as survival suffering is real. Comfort is a luxury bestowed on the privileged.

Man is curious by nature.

The imagination is vast creative beyond the manifestion of realisation.

Pre birth man visualised reincarnation.

While we live mankind is governed by karma of his sins. In truth Gravity is king.

Upon death without reasonable does the concept of manifest in the reality where there is no flesh, shadow, soul the spirit.

Perhaps God is testing our faith. Who do you put your faith in mankind or God?

When it is your time to go will you rest in peace? Will you be haunted by the bones of your reckless ways shadow of your sins..

Let Us Breed So WE Can Live Forever:

A Poem By

Nkosinathi 2Pistolz Ncala

The Conspiracy of The Sun:

The Sun Is A Mirror.

The Sun is a telepathic instrument an interface of the world reality and dreams. A thought remains a thought a dream remains a dream unless the thought it dreams leaves the mind and it comes alive.

Your perception of reality becomes the image our perception will perceive as our simulation. The danger of thought can not be undermined.

The image the consciousness the thought. The mind the environment the climatology. The soul the spirit the metaphysical. The past the present the future. The now the present the moment.

Wisdom understanding discerning the extraction of thought is a Calais who's depth measures nature of thought which is buried within consciousness.

Thinking without foreseen the reverse reaction is essentially blind in hind sight.

The Conspiracy of The Sun:

The sun is the shadow of existence.

The depth of the ocean.

On average the depth of the deepest part of the ocean is 10 kms in depth.

On land the highest mountain Himalayan

Is 8 kms in height.

The strength of the ocean tides is determined by the tiptronic plates thus the length frequency and intensity of the waves is determined underlined by the position of the moon.

Ok earth the seed is the womb.

The branch and the stem is the organism the flowers and the fruits carry the DNA of the seed. The soil is the consciousness the genealogy of all forms of life.

The cloud come with the rains.

Water is the source of all forms of life living with breath.

Water takes the form of a gas, liquid, solid. Water can only be heated using fire. Fire essentially comes from the sun.

What is the source of water clouds. We all know how clouds form precipitation.

The Conspiracy of The Sun:

The Sun Is A Mirror.

The Density of Thought:

The elaboration of the mass of thought.

Thought levitates on the axis of consciousness. The world of thought is undefined.

For who stipulates the nature of thoughts that will surface in the mind.

The frequency of thought is a balance of the equilibrium of thinking contemplating and a state of things as they are.

Only in reality can dreams manifest.

Nightmares are an indication that thought is disturbed. What would traumatise thought? Emotional psychological abuse which lead to financial dependence and domination.

Thought is scarred by memories that play over and over again in the mind reminding us of our milestones and pitfalls. Thought lives in the mind and in reality simultaneously.

Yet as long as the organism is alive.

Thought can not escape the simulation.

The magnitude and gratitude of grace is bestowed upon a multitude of unseen possibilities. Insight is angular to the perception of intention. The motive reveals what liveth in the heart, behold the naked mind.

How hollow is your faith?

Can the latitude of your hope summit a mountain? Is your fear is deep as the ocean, even if you can swim how long can you float? Doubt is riddled in anxiety.

Put your faith in tomorrow.

For today us all well really own?

Do you own your wealth?

Where is your inheritance stored?

What if the reserve Bank was to collapse? What if?

What is the frequency of thinking?

Two thoughts blinded by the ego.

An altercation accrues at the intersection of the mind. There are no casualties. Yet the battle was intense.

A bullock and a lamb.

Horns locked.

Blood is drawn.

All for the right to mate with the faiest sheep in the land.

Things we do for love.

The Density of Thought:

What Is Your Mind Worth?

What is you role in society?

What impact does your life have on the community? What is the relevence of your existence?

When all is said and done did you manifest your primary dream? If not. Why not? Is there time if so what are you doing about it?

A Poem By

Nkosinathi 2Pistolz Ncala

About the Author

Poet

From South Africa.

A diverse style of poetry

Influences of the following genra

Literature

Philosophy

Psychology

Philosophy

Read more at https://www.facebook.com/nkosinathi.ncala.16.